GERMANY, 1870–1945

GERMANY, 1870–1945

Politics, State Formation, and War

PETER PULZER
Gladstone Professor Emeritus
of Government
and
Public Administration,
University of Oxford

Oxford University Press

*This book has been printed digitally and produced in a standard specification
in order to ensure its continuing availability*

OXFORD
UNIVERSITY PRESS

Great Clarendon Street, Oxford OX2 6DP

Oxford University Press is a department of the University of Oxford.
It furthers the University's objective of excellence in research, scholarship,
and education by publishing world-wide in

Oxford New York

Auckland Bangkok Buenos Aires Cape Town Chennai
Dar es Salaam Delhi Hong Kong Istanbul Karachi Kolkata
Kuala Lumpur Madrid Melbourne Mexico City Mumbai Nairobi
São Paulo Shanghai Taipei Tokyo Toronto

Oxford is a registered trade mark of Oxford University Press
in the UK and in certain other countries

Published in the United States
by Oxford University Press Inc., New York

© Peter Pulzer 1997
The moral rights of the author have been asserted
Database right Oxford University Press (maker)

Reprinted 2003

ISBN 978-0-19-878135-6

FOR GILLIAN

once more with love
and gratitude

Acknowledgements

I have read more books about the history and politics of Germany in the nineteenth and twentieth centuries than I care to remember and discussed them, with pleasure and profit, with colleagues and students in three continents. Those who recognize their influences on me will, I hope, feel flattered rather than exploited and will find themselves duly mentioned in the Suggestions for Further Reading. I also hope that at least some of them have found the relationship to be reciprocal. I owe, as always, a particular debt to my wife, Gillian, for her meticulous proof-reading and stylistic vigilance; and to Michèle Jacottet, who prepared the text in her exemplary way.

Contents

Abbreviations

AEG   Allgemeine Elektrizitäts-Gesellschaft

BdI   Bund der Industriellen (League of Industrialists)

CDI   Centralverein Deutscher Industrieller (Central Association of German Industrialists)

DAF   Deutsche Arbeitsfront (German Labour Front)

DDP   Deutsche Demokratische Partei (German Democratic Party)

DHV   Deutschnationaler Handlungsgehilfen-Verband (German Nationalist Commercial Employees' Union)

DNVP   Deutschnationale Volkpartei (German Nationalist People's Party)

DVP   Deutsche Volkspartei (German People's Party)

KPD   Kommunistische Partei Deutschlands (German Communist Party)

SA   Sturm-Abteilungen (Storm Troopers, i.e. brownshirts)

SD   Sicherheitsdienst (Security Service)

SPD   Sozialdemokratische Partei Deutschlands (German Social Democratic Party)

SS   Schutz-Staffeln (Protection Squads, i.e. blackshirts)

USPD   Unabhängige Sozialdemokratische Partei Deutschlands (German Independent Social Democratic Party)

Chronology

1848	12–19 March	Revolutionary uprisings in major German cities
	18 May	National Assembly meets in Frankfurt
1849	28 March	Frankfurt National Assembly adopts constitution for Germany
	3 April	Imperial crown rejected by Friedrich Wilhelm IV of Prussia
1859	15–16 Sept.	Foundation of *Deutscher Nationalverein*
1861	6 June	Foundation of Progressive Party
1862	23 September	Bismarck appointed Prime Minister of Prussia
1866	3 July	Austrian army defeated at Königgrätz
1867	12 February	Election to Constituent Reichstag of North German Federation
1870	2 September	Prussian victory over France at Sedan
1871	18 January	Wilhelm I proclaimed German Emperor at Versailles
	16 April	Constitution of German Empire adopted
1873	9 May	Crash on Vienna stock exchange leads to depression in Germany
1873–4		*Kulturkampf* legislation reducing rights of clergy and introducing compulsory civil marriage
1876	1 January	Reichsbank established
1878	2 June	Second attempt on Emperor's life
	13 June–13 July	Bismarck presides over Congress of Berlin
	19 October	Anti-Socialist law passed
1879	12 July	Tariff legislation ends period of free trade
1880	30 August	Split in National Liberal Party ends parliamentary dominance of Liberalism
1881	17 November	Imperial message on programme of social legislation

1884	24 April	First German colony in Africa founded
1888	9 March	Death of Wilhelm I
	16 June	Death of Friedrich III, succeeded by Wilhelm II
1890	20 March	Bismarck resigns as Chancellor. Succeeded by Caprivi
1891–4		Caprivi signs treaties to liberalize foreign trade
1898	26 March	German naval law passed
1906	7 April	Algeciras Conference ends first Morocco crisis. German claims rejected
1908	28 October	*Daily Telegraph* publishes 'interview' with Emperor
1909	14 July	Bülow resigns as Chancellor. Succeeded by Bethmann Hollweg
1912	12–15 Jan.	SPD becomes strongest party in Reichstag elections
	7 February	Failure of Haldane mission to secure end to Anglo-German arms race
1914	28 June	Assassination of Archduke Franz Ferdinand of Austria in Sarajevo
1914	1 August	Germany declares war on Russia
	3 August	Germany declares war on France
	4 August	Great Britain declares war on Germany after German invasion of Belgium
1916	29 August	Hindenburg appointed Chief of General Staff and Ludendorff as Quartermaster-General
1917	1 February	Germany declares unrestricted submarine warfare
	6 April	USA declares war on Germany
	14 July	Bethmann Hollweg dismissed as Chancellor
	19 July	Reichstag passes peace resolution
	7 November	Bolshevik seizure of power in Russia
1918	8 January	President Wilson proclaims Fourteen Points
	3 March	Peace Treaty of Brest Litovsk with Russia
	8 August	Allied breakthrough on Western front

	21 September	Hindenburg and Ludendorff demand armistice negotiations
	29 October	Naval mutiny at Kiel
	7 November	Beginning of revolutionary movement in major cities
1918	9 November	German Republic proclaimed. Ebert (SPD) appointed Chancellor
	11 November	Armistice ends First World War
1919	15 January	Rosa Luxemburg and Karl Liebknecht murdered
	19 January	Election to Constituent Assembly at Weimar
	28 June	Peace Treaty signed at Versailles
	11 August	Constitution adopted at Weimar comes into force
1920	13 March	Kapp *putsch*
1922	16 April	Treaty of Rapallo between Germany and Soviet Union
	24 April	Rathenau murdered
1923	11 January	French and Belgian troops occupy the Ruhr
	September	Hyper-inflation peaks
	8 November	Attempted *putsch* by Hitler in Munich
	15 November	Stabilized Reichsmark introduced
1924	30 August	Dawes Plan on reparations schedule adopted
1925	26 April	Hindenburg elected President
	1 December	Locarno Treaty signed
1926	10 September	Germany joins League of Nations
1928	28 June	Grand Coalition under Hermann Müller (SPD)
1929	7 June	Young Plan to revise reparations schedule
	10 October	Death of Stresemann
	25 October	New York stock exchange crash
1930	29 March	Brüning leads minority government after collapse of Grand Coalition
	30 June	End of French occupation of Rhineland
	14 September	NSDAP breakthrough in Reichstag elections

1931	6 July	President Hoover orders moratorium on reparations payments
1932	10 April	Hindenburg re-elected President
	1 July	Papen succeeds Brüning as Chancellor
	20 July	Papen deposes SPD government of Prussia
	31 July	Reichstag elections. NSDAP becomes largest party
	2 December	Schleicher succeeds Papen as Chancellor
1933	30 January	Hitler appointed Chancellor
	28 February	'Reichstag Fire Decree'
	24 March	'Enabling Law' passed
	1 April	Boycott of Jewish shops
	20 July	Concordat with Vatican
	10 October	Germany leaves League of Nations
1934	20 April	Creation of 'People's Courts'
	30 June	'Night of long knives' against SA leadership
	2 August	Death of President Hindenburg. Hitler combines posts of President and '*Führer* and *Reich* Chancellor'
1935	16 March	Military conscription introduced
	15 September	Nuremberg racial laws proclaimed
1936	7 March	German army occupies Rhineland
	17 June	Himmler appointed head of German police
	29 October	Proclamation of Four Year Plan
1937	14 March	Papal encyclical 'Mit brennender Sorge'
	18 July	Exhibition of 'degenerate art' in Munich
1938	4 February	**Hitler becomes Commander-in-Chief of Army** after dismissal of Blomberg and Fritsch
	12 March	German troops occupy Austria
	29 September	Munich agreement partitions Czechoslovakia
	9 November	'Kristallnacht' pogrom
1939	15–16 March	German troops occupy Prague. Creation of Protectorate of Bohemia and Moravia
	31 March	Anglo-French guarantee to Poland

	23 August	Germany and Soviet Union sign Non-Aggression Pact
	1 September	German attack on Poland
	3 September	Britain and France declare war on Germany
	October	'Euthanasia' programme initiated
1940	9 April	German forces invade Denmark and Norway
	10 May	German army opens offensive against France, Belgium and Netherlands
1940	22 June	Franco-German armistice
	August–Sept.	Battle of Britain
1941	6 April	Germany launches offensive against Yugoslavia and Greece
	22 June	Invasion of Soviet Union
	11 December	Germany declares war on USA
1942	20 January	Wannsee Conference to co-ordinate the 'final solution of the Jewish Question'
	8 February	Speer appointed Minister for Armaments
	23 October–3 November	Battle of El Alamein
1943	14–25 Jan.	Casablanca Conference. Roosevelt and Churchill demand unconditional surrender of Germany
	31 January	German 6th Army surrenders at Stalingrad
	18 February	Goebbels's 'total war' speech
	25 July	Overthrow of Mussolini. End of Fascist regime in Italy
1944	6 June	Allied landings in Normandy
	20 July	Attempt on Hitler's life
	25 September	Conscription of all men between 16 and 60
1945	4–11 Feb.	Yalta Conference. Roosevelt, Churchill and Stalin decide on post-war government of Germany
	19 March	Hitler orders policy of scorched earth
	30 April	Suicide of Hitler. Admiral Doenitz becomes head of government
	8 May	Capitulation of German armed forces.

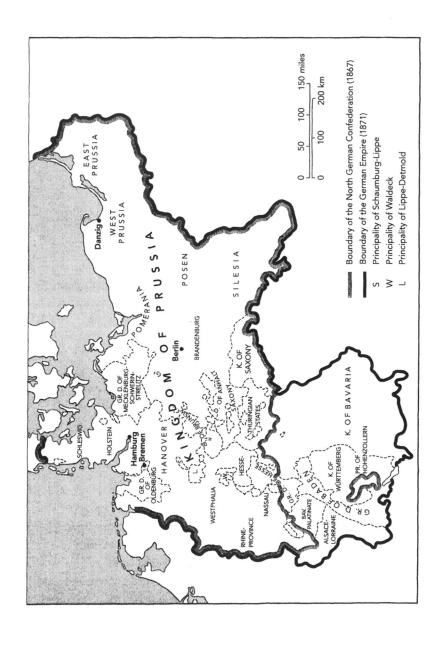

EAST PRUSSIA

WEST PRUSSIA

Danzig

POMERANIA

POSEN

SILESIA

KINGDOM OF PRUSSIA

Berlin

BRANDENBURG

K. OF SAXONY

SCHLESWIG

HOLSTEIN

GR. D. OF MECKLENBURG-SCHWERIN-STRELITZ

Hamburg Bremen

GR. D. OF OLDENBURG

HANOVER

D. OF ANHALT

SAXONY

THURINGIAN STATES

WESTPHALIA

HESSE

HESSE

RHINE-PROVINCE

NASSAU

BAV. PALATINATE

ALSACE-LORRAINE

GR. D. OF BADEN

K. OF WÜRTTEMBERG

PR. OF HOHENZOLLERN

K. OF BAVARIA

Boundary of the North German Confederation (1867)

Boundary of the German Empire (1871)

S Principality of Schaumburg-Lippe

W Principality of Waldeck

L Principality of Lippe-Detmold

0   50   100   150 miles
0   100   200 km

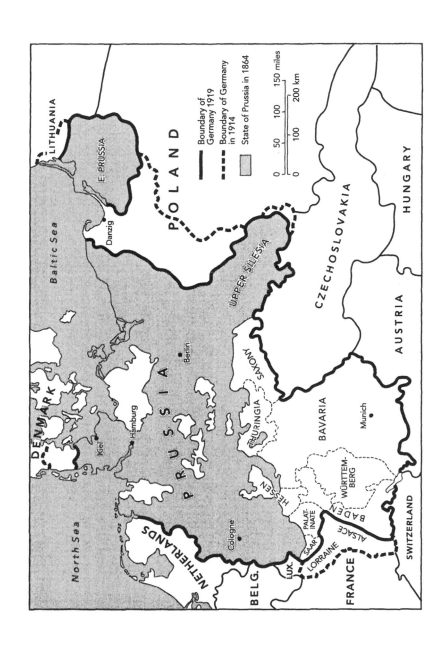

LITHUANIA

POLAND

E. PRUSSIA

Danzig

Baltic Sea

UPPER SILESIA

CZECHOSLOVAKIA

HUNGARY

AUSTRIA

Berlin

SAXONY

DENMARK

PRUSSIA

Hamburg

Kiel

THURINGIA

BAVARIA

Munich

HESSEN

WÜRTTEM-
BERG

BADEN

PALAT-
INATE

North Sea

NETHERLANDS

Cologne

SAAR

ALSACE

LORRAINE

SWITZERLAND

BELG.

LUX.

FRANCE

Boundary of
Germany 1919

Boundary of Germany
in 1914

State of Prussia in 1864

0   50   100   150 miles

0   100   200 km

Introduction

This book is intended to be a companion to my earlier *German Politics, 1945–1995*. My aim in both books is to emphasize both the continuities and the breaks in the German political experience of the last century and a half. Above all, I try to show the significance of the disintegration of the German state in 1945 in both its causes and its consequences. All authors have to make hard choices about what to put in and what to leave out. There is much in German local and associational politics and in social development that is fascinating, but would have distracted from a narrative that aims to highlight the broad lines of development—the national movement, state structures and constitutions, parties and pressure groups, public opinion and popular participation, the economy, diplomacy, military planning and the conduct of war. There is now such a wealth of monographs on so many aspects of German political life—not all of them available in English—that to do justice to them all would have been impossible. I have tried to give a balanced indication of many of these topics in the Suggestions for Further Reading.

1 The Road to Unity

> The great decisions of our time will not be made by speeches and majority resolutions—that was the great mistake of 1848 and 1849—but by iron and blood.
>
> (Otto von Bismarck, 30 September 1862)

For most of the nineteenth century three overlapping issues dominated the political debate in Germany. The first concerned national identity, the second the rivalries of the various German dynasties, the third the claims of popular self-government. Neither at the beginning nor at the end of the century were there agreed answers to the questions that these debates raised.

Who was a German, and what did it mean to be a German? Romantic poets gave ambiguous answers. For Ernst Moritz Arndt, writing during the Napoleonic Wars, Germany was to be found 'wherever the German tongue resounds'. August Heinrich Hoffmann von Fallersleben, in a poem that was later to become the German national anthem, defined his 'Deutschland'—no more than a geographical expression at that time—rather generously as stretching from present-day Belgium to present-day Lithuania and present-day Northern Italy to the Baltic Sea. At this stage—that is to say, at any time before 1848—Germans were defined in cultural terms. A German was anyone who was born to a German-speaking family, whether from one of the states within the German Confederation that was created in 1815, or from one of the German settler colonies in Eastern Europe, for instance those in Romania, the Russian Empire, or the southern and eastern regions of the Habsburg Monarchy, in present-day Hungary and Serbia. This linguistic definition of national identity, that of the *Kulturnation*, differed from the notion of citizenship in the established nation-states of Western Europe, such as France and Britain. There the criteria of birth and residence took precedence over those of ancestry and the nation consisted of those who were the citizens of the state, irrespective of language or parentage: they constituted a *Staatsnation*, a political nation. Thus one part of the public agenda of nineteenth-century Germany was to devise a way of turning the *Kulturnation* into a *Staatsnation*.

Such a process would require popular participation and would therefore challenge the political settlement that reorganized German-speaking Europe after the defeat of Napoleon. This was based on a return to the principle of monarchical legitimacy that the French Revolution and Napoleon had undermined. Not all the multiplicity of states that had existed before 1789 were restored; there were, however, still thirty-nine of them, with the Kingdom of Prussia and the Austrian Empire at one end of the scale and petty principalities like Schaumburg-Lippe and Schwarzburg-Sondershausen at the other. They were loosely bound together in the German Confederation, whose frontiers more or less followed those of the Holy Roman Empire that Napoleon had abolished in 1806. The Confederation was German only in an approximate way. The eastern provinces of Prussia, though containing a sizeable German population, lay outside it; and though only the western half of the Austrian Empire was inside it, this contained large Czech, South Slav, and Italian minorities. Neither in its ethnic composition nor in the internal constitutions of the member states did it respect the principle of self-determination, and the sense of nationhood that had been so effectively mobilized in the struggle against Napoleon was once more at a discount. German nationalism, whether as an abstract sentiment or a concrete political programme, could flourish only at the expense of monarchical legitimacy. For that reason it was viewed with either suspicion or downright hostility by all of Germany's rulers, most of all by the most powerful politician in the Confederation, the Austrian chief minister, Prince Metternich. For the whole of the Metternich era, that is to say from the restorations of 1815 to the outbreak of the revolutions in 1848, the cause of nation-building was also the cause of subversion. Those who sought political unity for all Germans were in general Liberals or Democrats who also sought, if not popular sovereignty, then at least government by consent. But the association of the national cause with that of general emancipation was always somewhat uneasy. The advocate of national liberation sees many enemies. The foreign occupying power, as in the days of Napoleonic domination, is one. The absolute monarch who denies the claims of the people is another. But so are external foes, real or imagined, whether in the form of a military threat or of cultural superiority. And so, above all, are enemies within—groups or individuals who challenge the homogeneity of the nation or deny the primacy of the national over all other criteria of state organization. Johann Gottlieb Fichte gave an early indication of the authoritarian side of the ideology of nationalism in his *Addresses to the German Nation*, which he delivered in 1807 and 1808, just after Napoleon's most crushing victories. 'The first, original, and truly natural frontiers of all states', he asserted, 'are undoubtedly their inner frontiers'. This was a common theme. Fichte's contemporary, Friedrich Ludwig Jahn, the founder of the patriotic gymnasts' movement, insisted that a true people, a 'genuine *Volk*' would 'maintain its outward community of state through the force of internal links'. Jahn was in no doubt who the external and internal enemies of the German people were: 'Frenchmen, Junkers, priests, and Jews'. So, too, Fichte declared that the German *Volk* had to subsist 'without interference from and ruination by anything foreign'. This anti-pluralist, monocultural form of nationalism reached its first climax in the struggle against Napoleon, but its xenophobia, directed especially against anything French, was never absent and revived as the century wore on.

The first test of the relative strengths of these various ideological tendencies came in the revolutions of 1848. They were triggered by the outburst of revolutionary violence in Paris at the end of February, though the way had been prepared in the short term by widespread economic distress and in the longer term by the emergence of an organized Liberal movement, demanding constitutional reform and greater national cohesion. The revolutions in the major cities of the Confederation—Berlin, Vienna, Prague, Munich, and Dresden— were in the first place directed against the Metternich system of autocracy and repression. The demands of the revolutionaries were for freedom of the press and of assembly, popular militias, and representative government. After the barricades and street-battles of the March days, the moderate Liberal movement, led by the educated middle class, gained the upper hand; far from wishing to overthrow the dynasties, it sought reforms on the basis of compromise. Through the spring and summer of 1848 uprisings, demanding radical democratization and even Socialist redistribution of property, punctuated parliamentary deliberations. At an early stage they marked the dividing line between reformers and revolutionaries that was to reappear later in the century.

It was at this stage that the divergent interests of the various German states, in particular of Austria and Prussia, became evident. The King of Prussia and his ministers, hostile though they were to any notions of popular sovereignty, could, if they so chose, associate themselves with the notion of German unity. Prussia was an overwhelmingly German state and had, indeed, taken a first step in claiming leadership of the unity movement with the creation of a customs union of German states—the *Zollverein* of 1834—which excluded Austria. Austria, on the other hand, which dominated the politics of the Confederation from 1815 to 1848, was committed to the *status quo*. It was a multinational state and the revolutions that broke out in its Italian-, Hungarian-, and Czech-speaking regions demanded independence, or at least autonomy, from Vienna. Austria could remain the leading German power only if the monarchical principle prevailed over the national. If, on the other hand, the national principle prevailed, the Austrian Empire would cease to exist as a state.

These divergent responses to the challenge of German nationalism were highlighted by the proceedings of the National Assembly, elected in May. It met in Frankfurt, and was therefore often referred to as the Frankfurt Parliament. It set itself the task of drawing up a constitution for a united, democratic Germany and, in the meantime, to nominate a provisional government. The choice for the president of the provisional government, the Habsburg Archduke Johann, reflected the old balance of power; the debates in the National Assembly demonstrated the difficulties in creating a new one. These difficulties related first to the question of frontiers and secondly to the question of sovereignty.

It was one thing to declare a united Germany as an aim, another to decide what it should include. Here the hyperboles of the Romantic poets helped little. In the North the duchies of Schleswig and Holstein, populated by a majority of Germans and a minority of Danes, declared for inclusion in a future Germany, but the government of Prussia, which alone could have lent reality to this wish, feared the adverse reaction of the European powers and left well alone. In the East the National Assembly insisted on the inclusion of all areas of mixed German–Polish population, bequeathing a legacy of distrust and hatred that lasted through the rest of the century and beyond. In the South-East and South it insisted on including all those Habsburg territories that had lain within the Confederation, thus disregarding the claims of the Italian and Czech populations for self-determination. An inescapable truth had dawned: that a state designed to include all Germans would have to include a great many non-Germans, too. The simple slogan of 'unity and liberty' ignored the liberty, and in some cases the unity, of others.

Side by side with the problem of frontiers, that of sovereignty proved equally insoluble. Prussia's passivity in the Schleswig-Holstein dispute had shown that as long as the separate German states continued to exist, the National Assembly's resolutions were empty words. The same applied to the provisional government's decree that the armies of the various states should swear allegiance to Archduke Johann; most of them failed to do so. Nor did the National Assembly have more luck in its attempts to finance itself and its provisional government with contributions from the states. It did proceed, however slowly, to draw up a constitution for a united Germany, beginning with a Bill of Rights which, though never implemented, remained as part of the German public agenda. The attempts to complete the draft foundered on the familiar questions of frontiers, which cut across the Prussian–Austrian rivalry.

Not only did the Austrian Government see in the programme of German unification a threat to its predominance in Germany; it saw in the other national revolutions a threat to its existence. To crush these revolutions with military means was therefore a matter of much greater urgency for Austria than for Prussia. With the aid of Russian armies the new Habsburg Emperor Franz Joseph put an end to the insurgency in October. The prospect of a Greater German solution to the question of unity, i.e. one that included the Habsburg territories, was thereby eliminated. What remained was the Lesser German option, i.e. under the patronage of Prussia. This had always seemed the more plausible of the two, since some form of German unification was not inherently incompatible with Prussian state interests. It had gained all the more plausibility in March 1848 when King Friedrich Wilhelm IV, a man of strongly Romantic disposition, had appeared in public draped in the German national colours of black, red, and gold and declared that Prussia would 'henceforth be absorbed in Germany'. But by the time a delegation from the National Assembly offered him the German Imperial Crown on 3 April 1849 he had changed his mind and declined a diadem sullied by 'the stench of revolution'. The monarchical cause, which had won its first victory in Vienna, was on the way to recovery; the National Assembly dispersed in humiliation, having discovered that covenants without the sword are but words. The Confederation of 1815 was restored, but those who ruled it could not act as if nothing had happened.

The events of 1848 and 1849, tragicomical though some of them were, left lasting legacies. The first of these was that the cause of German national unity was now on the public agenda and unlikely to go away. The second was that the first national parliament in German history, and the first attempt to solve the national question by parliamentary means, was discredited. Nothing would now be easier than to dismiss parliaments as ineffectual talking shops and the disdain in which elected institutions were held was to prove a baneful element in German public life. The third was that the Liberal reformers of the Frankfurt Parliament distrusted and even feared the people. The various violent risings that punctuated the spring of 1848, not to mention the beginnings of a workers' movement, reminded many of the parliamentarians of the fate of the sorcerer's apprentice, who had released spirits that he could no longer control. The prospects for a national movement on a democratic basis were thereby diminished. The fourth was that a satisfactory definition of German nationality and of German national territory was more elusive than the Romantic evocations of earlier decades had suggested. The Frankfurt Parliament's disregard for the claims of Danish, Czech, Polish, and Italian nationalists suggested that German aspirations could be fulfilled only at the expense of their neighbours'. Lastly it emerged that while the interests of Prussia might under certain circumstances be reconciled with the cause of German unity, those of Austria depended on the maintenance of the monarchical order of 1815. Any revival of German nationalist sentiment would therefore reawaken the competition between Prussia and

Austria for dominance in Germany. This was indeed to happen within ten years.

In the meantime, however, Prussia and Austria consolidated the defeat of the Revolution. Their actions had shown that as long as the individual states retained control of their armies, parliamentary hot air counted for nothing. It followed from this that the reconstruction of Germany could proceed only on the initiative of one of the leading German powers—or at the very least could not proceed against their opposition. The first stage of the restoration of 1849–50, however, was a settlement of the scores not only with the revolutionaries, but between Austria and Prussia. Austria was determined not only to repress the nationalist movement and the demands for popular sovereignty, but to reassert its primacy within the Confederation. It therefore moved sternly to interdict moves by Friedrich Wilhelm to form an 'inner union' of German states, the so-called Erfurt Union, that would exclude Austria and enhance the dependence of the smaller and middle states on Prussia. Once the last rebellions in Austria had been crushed, it imposed on Prussia, at the 'Punctation of Olmütz' on 29 November 1850, the unqualified acceptance of the old order.

Though the old order was now back in place, its foundations had been weakened. For a decade public opinion was quiescent, but once it reasserted itself the agenda interrupted in 1849 was resumed. Above all, not all the relics of the Revolution were suppressed. Most of the German states retained the constitutions that had been won in 1848–9, or decreed in the aftermath of 1849. Though these were far from democratic, they ensured some forms of representative government and provided some public debate. In addition to parliaments some of the press survived. Despite censorship, this, too, kept some kind of political life going.

By 1859 German political activity had well and truly revived. The immediate impetus for this came from the wars of Italian unification that relit the flame of European nationalism and resulted in the proclamation of the Kingdom of Italy in 1860. But that was only the proximate cause. Longer-term factors were also at work. Economic dynamism and industrialization, already under way before 1848, accelerated. The expansion of intra-German and foreign trade, the improvement of communications, whether through railway construction or the creation of the German Postal Union in 1850, made the manifold frontiers between the states less and less relevant to the realities of daily life. Moreover, this economic growth was largely restricted to the members of the *Zollverein*. Austria was therefore excluded from the benefits of the economic trends, just as it was weakened militarily and diplomatically through its defeats in Italy in 1859. A further factor favouring the reopening of the German Question was internal political change in Prussia. In 1858 Prince Wilhelm succeeded the mentally ill Friedrich Wilhelm IV, first as Regent, then as King and embarked on a cautious liberalizing course, known as the 'New Era'. In 1859 a number of Liberal politicians and journalists, many of them veterans of 1848, formed the *Deutscher Nationalverein*, with the aim of reviving the scheme of a Prussian-led Lesser Germany. Two years later the Prussian activists of this body created the Progressive Party on a parliamentary and electoral basis. Though both these bodies had a radical-democratic wing, they were dominated by middle-class moderates, who had learned the lesson of 1848–9 that limited aims and realistic methods were most likely to lead to success. The bourgeois character of the new Liberal formations also fitted the graded Prussian franchise, which favoured taxpayers over non-taxpayers and higher over lower taxpayers.

With the re-emergence of political debate and the change of guard in Prussia, the familiar fault-lines of German politics reappeared. In response to the pro-Prussian *Nationalverein*, the *Deutscher Reformverein* was founded, to advocate a more loosely federated Greater German solution to the question of unity, a proposal much more to the liking of Austria and to the governments of many of the medium and smaller states. Thus the Prussian–Austrian rivalry once more set the tone in the debate on the reshaping of Germany. The other conflict that these competing formations ignited was that between governments and public opinion. A Greater German federation appealed to those in power; a Lesser German, more centralized solution to those out of power. That did not mean, however, that the Prussian Liberals and the Prussian government saw eye to eye. The leaders of the Progressive Party and of the *Nationalverein* remembered the role of the Prussian army in crushing the Revolution in 1849. They concluded from this that constitutional reform in Prussia, and above all parliamentary control of the army, was a precondition of German unity and on the basis of that programme they won a series of impressive electoral victories.

Parliamentarization of the army was, however, precisely what the new King of Prussia was not prepared to tolerate. To resist and defeat the Progressives' demands he appointed Count Otto von Bismarck to head the government. Bismarck saw that German national sentiment might be exploited to ensure Prussia's advantage over Austria, but had no doubt about his favoured instrument for pursuing this, or any other objective. 'The great decisions of our time', he declared on entering office, were decided 'not by speeches and majority decisions . . . but by iron and blood'. 'Germany', he claimed, 'looks not to Prussia's Liberalism, but to Prussia's might'. Iron and blood were indeed to dominate the 1860s, leading Bismarck to victory over his external enemies and domestic opponents. Yet it would be a mistake to assume that there was an unalterable logic to this chain of events or that Bismarck embarked on his tenure of office with a fully formed game plan. Though the solution he imposed on the German Question shaped German politics for three generations, this was due as much to the way he manipulated the various forces that stood in his way as to the form of the outcome.

Iron and blood played their part on three occasions, though by themselves they could not have produced the outcome that they did. The first occasion arose through a contingency—the decision of the Danish parliament in 1863 to separate the disputed duchies of Schleswig and Holstein and incorporate Schleswig in a unitary Denmark. This enraged German nationalist opinion, which remembered the humiliation of 1848 and favoured the inclusion of the duchies in a united Germany under the Dukes of Augustenburg. Bismarck's response was an earnest of his favoured tactics. In accordance with the principles of European monarchism he supported the Danish crown against Augustenburg; in protest against the Danish parliament's unilateral action a Prussian-Austrian army moved into Schleswig and Holstein, defeated the Danish army, and jointly occupied the duchies on behalf of the German Confederation. German Liberal opinion was outraged by Bismarck's arbitrariness, his Machiavellianism, and his decision to make Schleswig-Holstein an object of monarchical manœuvres, rather than turn it into a self-determined German state within the Confederation. Above all it was outraged by its own impotence.

The second occasion was a dispute between Prussia and Austria over the administration of the Danish duchies, which led to a Prussian invasion of Austrian-occupied Holstein. When the German Confederation condemned this action, Prussia declared the Confederation at an end and invaded Austria. Less than two weeks later Austria was decisively defeated at Königgrätz. At the Peace of Prague that concluded the war, Austria acknowledged the end of the Confederation and her exclusion from the affairs of Germany. With future diplomatic needs in mind, Bismarck left the territory of the Habsburg Monarchy intact, but had no compunction in annexing Schleswig-Holstein or a number of Austria's allies in the recent war, including the Kingdom of Hanover, two Hessian states, and the Free City of Frankfurt-on-Main. Within four years of becoming Prime Minister, Bismarck had settled that part of the German Question that was at the top of Prussia's priorities—the rivalry with Austria for the dominant role in Germany. In doing so, he had also gone a long way towards settling that part of it that most concerned the politicians of the nationalist movement—but without consulting them and against their presumed wishes. Speeches and majority decisions had once more not prevailed.

With Austria excluded, the structure of Germany could be refashioned under the aegis of Prussia, but this related as much to the internal politics of the German states as to the map of Europe. When Prussia invaded Austria the Prussian constitutional conflict over control of the army was not yet resolved; the government's financing of the war was therefore illegal. The Liberal majority in the Prussian Parliament feared Bismarck for two reasons—they suspected that his government intended to use the army for internal repression and that he had no intention of bringing forward German unification. On the first their suspicions were justified, on the second he outwitted them. The Liberals wanted to subordinate the Prussian army in order to unify Germany. Bismarck unified Germany in order to preserve the Prussian army.

When Bismarck handed the German Liberals the victory of Königgrätz on a plate, they were faced with an agonizing dilemma.

The old order was overthrown and the Austrian veto over German self-determination was no more. These developments they could not but welcome. But the victory had been won in breach of the constitution and of international law. This was more difficult to swallow. The Prussian army remained—indeed, was confirmed—as the arbiter of the destiny of Germany. This was more difficult still to swallow. What Bismarck's *fait accompli* did was to split the Liberals. The majority of them followed the logic of the self-criticism by Hermann Baumgarten, the influential editor of the *Preußische Jahrbücher*:

Now that we have seen that these much-reviled Junkers know how to fight and die for the fatherland, the best Liberals notwithstanding, we shall have to tone down our bourgeois conceit a little and modestly maintain an honourable place beside the aristocracy. We thought that we would turn the German world upside down with our agitation; as it is, all we achieved was to make ourselves superfluous: I think we shall take these experiences to heart.

When the Prussian Parliament was asked to indemnify the government for its breach of the constitution, most Liberal members voted for the indemnity. They separated themselves from the old Progressive Party and formed themselves into the National Liberal Party. Only an irreconcilable minority remained true to their original principles. Recognizing that German revolutions come, if they are to be successful, from above, the National Liberals decided to make the most of their opportunities in post-Königgrätz Germany.

The first opportunity came with the creation of the North German Confederation, consisting of the now-enlarged Prussia and all other German states north of the River Main—i.e. excluding only Bavaria, Württemberg, Baden, and the southern part of the Grand Duchy of Hesse. The Confederation's parliament, the Reichstag, was elected by universal male suffrage in accordance with the electoral law devised by the Frankfurt Parliament in 1849. This suited Bismarck, who assumed that both Liberalism and nationalism were restricted to the middle class and that the predominantly rural masses, if enfranchised, would swamp them—a calculation that proved only partly right. The constitution for the North German Confederation that the Reichstag adopted showed what kind of compromise was now possible—indeed, inescapable—between a militarily victorious league of states, led by Prussia, and a chastened, but not beaten, Liberal movement. The democratic franchise, which most Liberals did not like, stayed in place. Nor did the Liberals secure a federal cabinet responsible to the Reichstag. But they did secure parliamentary control over the civilian budget and the promise of parliamentary control over the military budget. Of the greatest significance for the further development of Germany was the clause that permitted the adhesion of the remaining southern states. The adhesion did not have to wait long. Under pressure from Bismarck the southern states, which still belonged to the *Zollverein*, elected representatives, once more by universal male suffrage, to sit with the Reichstag of the North German Federation as a Customs Parliament (*Zollparlament*)—a legislature without a state. What triggered the completion of the process was the third military occasion by which Prussia's aggrandizement was concluded, the war with France in 1870 over the succession to the Spanish throne. The southern states, which had fought against Prussia in 1866, now joined the war on Prussia's side in accordance with the treaties they had signed after Königgrätz. A month after the outbreak of the war, on 2 September, the French army was crushed at Sedan and the southern states acceded to the North German Confederation even before Paris had fallen.

The Franco–Prussian War accelerated the work of unification, but was not decisive in bringing it about. The die was cast in 1866, when the defeat of Austria swept away all the other options that had been on the table. Prussian statecraft and military superiority determined the outcome; had the fortunes of war gone another way, the modern history of Germany would have been different. But Prussian statecraft did not operate in a vacuum. It made sense only in a long-maturing ideological context. The growth of German national sentiment was a fact, in accordance with Europe-wide trends and the accelerating urbanization and modernization of German society. Sooner or later the *Kulturnation* would also become a *Staatsnation*. The question was not whether, but when and how. Of the three issues we identified at the beginning, only one was decided by 1870. Königgrätz had permanently denied Austria the political leadership of Germany. As for who was a German, we have seen that no set of frontiers could provide an agreed answer to the conflicting claims of identity. Nor, as the formation of the North German Confederation had shown and the history of the Empire was to confirm, was there consensus on the place of the citizen in the state.

All the same, the events of 1870–1 marked a break. On 18 January 1871, four months after the Prussian victory at Sedan, in the Hall of Mirrors at Versailles, Wilhelm I of Prussia was crowned *Deutscher Kaiser*. For many Germans, the coronation symbolized a political coming of age. At last they, too, were citizens of that most modern of political forms, the European nation-state. What Englishmen and Frenchmen, Swedes and Spaniards had been able to take for granted for centuries, what even Italians had achieved in the preceding decade, Germans, too, could now claim as their own. This is certainly what the Reichstag of the North German Confederation had in mind when it called on Wilhelm 'to consecrate the work of unification by accepting the German Imperial Crown'.

2 Bismarck's Empire, 1871–1890

> This war represents the German revolution, a greater political
> event than the French revolution of the last century.
>
> (Benjamin Disraeli, House of Commons, 9 February 1871)
>
> A great victory is a great danger. Human nature endures it with
> greater difficulty than a defeat; indeed, it seems to be easier to
> achieve such a victory than to endure it in such a way that it does
> not result in a more severe defeat.
>
> (Friedrich Nietzsche, *David Strauß. Confessor and Writer*,
> 1873)

The Empire proclaimed at Versailles was born of military triumph and
subsumed the hopes of two generations of nationalist publicists. Yet
beneath the euphoria that accompanied the coronation there remained
ambiguities and doubts. Both the structure and the public symbols of
the new state left many dissatisfied. This was not merely because any
major innovation falls short of what its most ardent supporters hoped
for, while it intensifies the regrets of those who are attached to the past.
The out-and-out opponents of the new state were initially few. More
seriously, it emerged in the long run that its out-and-out supporters
were also few.

What sort of a *Reich* was this, and what sort of a *Kaiser?* The
words conjured up memories of medieval universality. They would
appeal—so Bismarck hoped in reviving them—to the traditionalists
who feared the revolutionary implications of the doctrine of national
self-determination. The new Emperor accepted his crown not by
popular acclaim, nor by a parliamentary resolution, but from the
hands of the Grand Duke of Baden. He was *Deutscher Kaiser*, the
emperor of a people, not *Kaiser Deutschlands*, the emperor of a territory, which would have implied sovereignty over the other kings and

princes of the German states. The Empire itself was created by treaty. The South German states had acceded individually to the North German Confederation; Bavaria only after a last-ditch stand in parliament by the anti-Prussian Patriotic Party. Yet it needed considerable powers of self-deception to believe that the Empire of 1871 was a revival of the one that had expired in 1806, or that Wilhelm I was in any except the most nominal way the successor of Charles V or Frederick Barbarossa. It was a new state decked out with old names.

The structure of the Empire reflected the way it had been created. It represented the promise rather than the achievement of the nation-state that the Liberals had hoped for. The new state lacked many of the elementary symbols of a unified people. The constitution contained no ringing, emotive appeal to the populace: it had not been drawn up, as had that of the United States, 'to establish justice, insure domestic tranquillity . . . promote the general welfare, and secure the blessings of liberty to ourselves and posterity'. There was no national holiday, like Bastille Day in France: 18 January was celebrated in Prussia only. There was, amazingly enough, no Imperial flag: it was only in 1892 that the naval and mercantile black-white-and-red was promoted to this status. (Black and white were the Prussian colours, red the colour of the Hanseatic cities.) There was no national anthem: 'Deutschland, Deutschland über alles'—Hoffmann von Fallersleben's revolutionary lyric set to Haydn's Imperial anthem—was not adopted until 1922. Though the developments of the years 1866 to 1871 undoubtedly enjoyed majority support, perhaps even enthusiasm, they also represented a victory of the military arm over the civilian, of autocracy over parliament, and of Prussia over its rivals and opponents in German-speaking Central Europe. The constitution of the Empire, accepted by the newly elected Reichstag on 16 April 1871, differed little from that of its predecessor, the North German Confederation. It was an 'eternal union' of the rulers of the constituent states. It was a federation, though a highly asymmetrical one. It contained elements of democracy, limited monarchy, and autocracy. It remained in force, unamended, until almost the end of the First World War, though by then the conflicts inherent in its contradictory provisions had become unmanageable.

The democratic element was the Reichstag, elected, like that of the North German Confederation, by full adult male suffrage. The element of limited monarchy lay in the relationship between the Emperor and the chief minister, the Chancellor, and the considerable prerogatives that the two possessed. The autocratic element lay in the Emperor's all but unqualified control of military and diplomatic affairs. Dominating all three of these components was the federal character of the Empire, which underlined the continuities in political structures that straddled the events of 1871. The twenty-five states that made up the new Empire retained their existing constitutions that dated in the main from the post-revolutionary period of 1849–50. Some of these, like those of Baden and Bavaria, were relatively liberal and others less so. The Grand Duchies of Mecklenburg-Schwerin and Mecklenburg-Strelitz were still governed by the Estates Settlement granted in 1775, i.e. fourteen years before the French Revolution. Until 1918 these two states had no elected parliaments. The parliaments of the other states were all elected by restricted franchises. Typical of these was the three-class franchise of Prussia in which voting power was determined by tax obligation. The highest taxpayers (about 5 per cent of all electors), the middle taxpayers (about 10 per cent), and the lowest taxpayers (the remaining 85 per cent) each elected one-third of the parliament. In many of the constituencies east of the River Elbe the local landowner, as the chief taxpayer, was the only elector in the first class and thus had one-third of the votes. In the city of Essen the head of the firm of Krupp enjoyed the same privilege. There was no secret ballot and representation was indirect—the voters of the three classes elected an electoral college, which then chose the members of parliament.

The states exercised their power in the Upper House of the Imperial parliament, the Bundesrat. Prussia, with 17 seats out of 58, had the largest delegation, which was almost always enough to ensure that it got its way. More importantly, since 14 votes were enough to block any constitutional amendment, Prussia had an absolute veto in this respect. That Prussia, with three-fifths of the total population, should dominate the new *Reich* was not surprising; it was even less surprising that this should be so, given the role of Prussia in creating it. What was significant was that this dominance was exercised by Old Prussia, unreformed and determined to stay so.

The constitution defined the powers of the different branches of government, but was silent on some of the realities of power. The democratic element, the Reichstag, was far from powerless. All Imperial legislation needed its assent, as did the annual Imperial budget. After much wrangling, so did the military budget, which initially accounted for nearly 90 per cent of Imperial expenditure, though this needed to be passed only every seven years. There were, however, limits to the Reichstag's powers. The Chancellor was required to explain his policies to the Reichstag, but it could not remove him from office; he was the Emperor's appointee, not that of parliament. Nor was there an Imperial government, with departmental ministers answerable to the Reichstag. A collective cabinet of this kind would have undermined the sovereignty of the constituent states, as would the Reichstag's control over such a cabinet. In so far as the Empire had a government, this was the Bundesrat, in which the Chancellor presided over the delegates of the state governments. As the responsibilities of the *Reich* expanded, administrative departments (*Reichsämter*) were created to deal with, *inter alia*, justice, finance, naval matters, and foreign affairs. By 1918 there were eleven of these. They were directed not by full ministers, but by state secretaries, strictly subordinate to the Chancellor. Moreover, they were recruited, more often than not, from among the Prussian delegates to the Bundesrat. There was thus a multiple overlap in the holders of Imperial and Prussian offices. Not only was the King of Prussia *ex officio* Emperor, not only was the Chancellor generally also Prime Minister of Prussia and always Prussian Foreign Minister, but many of the state secretaries were members of the Prussian cabinet. The real potential for conflict therefore lay not so much between Reichstag and Chancellor, or between Reichstag and Bundesrat, but between the majority of the democratic Reichstag and the majority of the oligarchic Prussian parliament (Landtag). Not for nothing did constitutional commentators refer to the Prussian parliament as the unofficial second chamber of the *Reich*.

The most autocratic element of the Imperial structure related to peace and war. In all matters of domestic policy, the Emperor's acts required the Chancellor's counter-signature. While this measure fell well short of democratic control, it was a safeguard against irresponsible decisions. This safeguard did not apply to the making of treaties or declarations of war, which required only the assent of the Bundesrat. This was not difficult to obtain. The Emperor alone was commander of the armed forces in both peace and war; as King of Prussia he was commander of the Prussian army, which provided by far the biggest contingents and almost all the higher leadership. In 1883 the last remaining element of civilian control was removed when matters of personnel in Prussia were transferred from the Minister of War, who might be subjected to parliamentary questions in the Prussian Landtag, to the Military Cabinet that was answerable only to the King-Emperor. It was this exemption of the armed forces from any external scrutiny that set the German Empire apart from all of the constitutional and parliamentary states of Western Europe.

Imperfect though the representative institutions of Germany were, they were effective within their limits; exactly how effective would depend on the party composition produced by elections. The parties represented in the Reichstag of the 1870s and 1880s were of two types. There were those, on the one hand, which survived from the constitutional struggles and ideological debates of the previous decades. Though their spokesmen might claim to have 'the people' or 'the nation' behind them, they had a narrow organizational base. Conservative or Liberal, they were parties led by men of education and property, national or local notables who claimed the allegiance of their followers in the House or the constituencies through personal distinction or social status. Their organization was informal, their paid-up membership small; they might even lack a constitution or an official programme.

Much the most powerful of these was the National Liberal Party, created by those who in 1867 had accepted Bismarck's solution of the German Question. Beyond a desire for national unity and civil liberties there was little to keep the party together. It represented in the main the industrial and professional middle classes, those with the greatest material and emotional attachment to a united Germany. It was strongest in the Protestant areas of the middle and smaller states: two-thirds of its deputies sat for constituencies outside the pre-1866 frontiers of Prussia. Its leader, Rudolf von Bennigsen, was, significantly, a Hanoverian, untouched by the bitter constitutional conflict of Prussia.

To their left was the irreconcilable hard-core remnant of the Progressive Party, refusing to accept that might could be right, but with little to offer once might had been proved right. It retained much of its Prussian following, where memories of the army conflict died hard, and gained that of the South German Democrats and of freetraders in the major commercial centres. It had distinguished leaders, including the historian Theodor Mommsen and the pathologist Rudolf Virchow, but was doomed to an oppositional role and could rarely influence policy decisively.

Like the Liberals, the Conservatives were divided. In Prussia, east of the River Elbe, they were the party of the landowning Junkers. Loyal to the dynasty and to the values of the Prussian state, they were embittered against Bismarck who had, in their eyes, sold out to the Liberals and the middle classes, destroying the old, reliable soldier-state in favour of the vague, fashionable slogans of nationalism. Thanks to the electoral system, they were sure of their voice in the Prussian parliament, but in the Reichstag they counted for very little: in 1874 they held only 22 seats out of 397. Other Conservatives, like many of the Liberals, decided to make their peace with the new order. They were men not exclusively tied to the soil: aristocrats, like Guido Count Henckel von Donnersmarck, who had diversified into industry and finance, tycoons like Wilhelm von Kardorff who were all for the new, enlarged market that the *Reich* offered, but had no time for liberal questionings of the prerogatives of authority. This party, known as the Freikonservative in Prussia and as the Reichspartei in the Reichstag, supported Bismarck unconditionally: unlike the crustier Junkers they foresaw the *Reich* as 'the German extension of the Prussian monarchy'.

The individualist structure of all these parties meant that none of them stood for very clear-cut principles or interests. They might describe themselves as 'liberal' or 'conservative' or acquire labels like 'bourgeois' or 'aristocratic', yet the borderlines between them were uncertain. Personal taste, family tradition, regional peculiarity, electoral calculation: each or all of these might determine a citizen's allegiance. The National Liberals in particular divided into a right wing, increasingly nationalist and decreasingly liberal, often indistinguishable from the Reichspartei, and a left wing that did not want to break the last links with the Progressives.

No such ambiguities beset the newer parties, with their mass memberships and their popular roots, the parties of the Catholics and the industrial workers. Initially the workers' party was much the weaker of the two. German industrialization was still only beginning in the 1860s, and Socialists were split into factions. The founder of the German Labour movement had been Ferdinand Lassalle, the son of a Jewish merchant from Silesia, a Byronic figure who was killed in a duel in 1864. He dominated his party by personality, not organization; after his death, the followers of Marx, led by August Bebel and Wilhelm Liebknecht, gained the upper hand. The Social Democratic Party (SPD), founded in 1875, was nominally a fusion of the two groups, but the organizational superiority and ideological toughness of the Marxists had its predictable effect. By 1878, when Bismarck turned the force of the law against the new party, it had half a million voters, 10 per cent of the total.

The other mass party, the Catholic Zentrum, was the strangest of all the political formations of the Empire. The second half of the nineteenth century was throughout Europe a time when the political and intellectual influence of the Catholic Church was most strongly under attack, and when it began to organize its defence. Catholic parties of one kind or another arose in most European states with large Catholic electorates. In Germany, however, there were special circumstances, which had to do with both the make-up of the Catholic tradition and the manner of national unification.

The leading German Catholics of the post-Napoleonic period—the Rhenish ex-Jacobin Joseph Görres, who became Professor of History at Munich, or the convert Adam Müller, who settled in Vienna—had been Conservative Romantics, exalting traditional authority against the challenge of the Enlightenment and the French Revolution. They preferred 'particularism', the multiplicity of small states, on the grounds of territorial legitimacy, combined with a loose confederation under the aegis of Catholic Austria. But this preference did not permit a uniform attitude towards Church–state relations. In Austria or Bavaria the unity of throne and altar could be taken for granted. But elsewhere, notably in Prussia, where Protestants predominated, constitutionalism was the best guarantee of Catholic rights.

Already in the Frankfurt Parliament of 1848–9 there had been a Catholic faction led by Wilhelm von Ketteler, the Bishop of Mainz, and the theologian Ignaz Döllinger. Later, in the Prussian Landtag, there had been one to safeguard the parity of the two faiths under the Prussian administration. It was the defeat of Austria at Königgrätz that spelt the end of Catholic-dominated Greater Germany. 'The world stinks', the Catholic politician Hermann von Mallinckrodt recorded; and indeed any Lesser German solution put the Catholics in a minority. Prussianization filled them with dismay; the unilateral annexation of Schleswig-Holstein and Hanover by Prussia seemed sacrilege. The constitutions of the North German Federation, and then of the *Reich*, with their mundane, commercial concerns, and their silence on fundamental rights, confirmed their worst fears.

Given their concern for a Bill of Rights, Catholics might have been expected to find common ground with the Liberals. But the Liberals were secular, pro-capitalist, and, for the most part, Prussophile; their dominance of German politics in the Empire's first decade determined the character of the Zentrum. It was founded in 1870, at first in Prussia only, to defend the federal principle, the rights of religion, and the interests of traditional occupations—farmers, artisans, the old *Mittelstand*. Its leader was Ludwig Windthorst, a brilliant debater and tactician who had been a minister of the last King of Hanover until 1866. Of course, not only Catholics wanted to defend these interests, and the founders of the party hoped it would be interconfessional. But the religious cleavage of Germany was too deep for that and it remained *de facto* a Catholic party. This was its weakness, but also its strength. It limited the Zentrum's size, but gave it internal cohesion and an obedient following. Through the parish priests it reached into every village. Through the social consciousness of Bishop Ketteler and Adolf Kolping, with his journeymen's associations—there are still *Kolpingvereine* and *Kolpingshäuser* throughout Germany—it reached deep into the working class. Like the Social Democrats, the Zentrum had a strict organization and a ready-made mass following. The *Volksverein für das katholische Deutschland* reached half a million members before the First World War.

The fox, says the Greek proverb, knows many things, the hedgehog knows one big thing. The Zentrum was a political hedgehog.

Socially its following ranged from landowners to coal-miners, geographically it was strongest at the Empire's periphery—Silesia in the east, Bavaria in the south, the Rhineland in the west. It was heterogeneous in all except religion, and several times it threatened to fall apart.

The compromise on which the Empire of 1871 was built was fragile and one in which the forces of Liberalism were in the long run the losers. In the short run, however, the two leading parties to the compromise seemed, from their very different standpoints, to desire complementary ends: Bismarck, the Empire's first Chancellor, to assert the hegemony of Prussia as a great power in Central Europe, the Liberals to ensure not merely a German *Nationalstaat* but a German *Machtstaat* (a powerful state). Bismarck was no economist, but he realized that Germany's diplomatic credibility and military self-sufficiency rested on economic strength; the Liberals, speaking for industry, trade, and finance, saw in economic unity the road to wealth as well as to the fulfilment of their ideals.

Though the Liberal parties had failed in 1871 to complete their constitutional agenda, they had gained much besides the creation of an embryonic nation-state. Society was liberalized more effectively than the state; indeed, from the point of view of the social and economic development of Germany, 1871 was not a particularly significant date. The freeing of trade through the *Zollverein* had, after all, been the effective beginning of German unity. The economic union of the southern states with Prussia, through the Customs Parliament of 1868, had preceded the constitution of the Empire by three years. The industrial boom in Prussia since 1857, contrasting with the stagnation of Austria, was a major factor in Bismarck's success with the middle classes. One German economic historian has justly described 1866 as the victory of the North German *Thaler* over the South German *Gulden*. If Bismarck opposed the old federal structure because it circumscribed the influence of Prussia and inhibited his conduct of foreign policy, the Liberals saw that it ran counter to their economic ambitions. A centralized state with a uniform administrative code, in which contract counted for more than status, rationality for more than tradition, efficiency for more than maintenance of the social order—this symbolized and guaranteed what they strove for.

Bismarck acquiesced. Pass laws, restricting freedom of movement, were abolished. Guild certificates, restricting the right to ply a trade, were abolished. The usury laws were repealed. Weights and measures were unified on the metric system. A commission was set up to draft a new Civil Code. Though the enactment of this had to wait until 1896, it underlined the significance of creating a single, modern legal framework for the new Empire. The Reichsmark, linked to a fixed gold value, became the sole currency. The formation of joint-stock companies, whose shares could be freely bought and sold on stock exchanges, was made easier. Import duties on unprocessed and semifinished metals were abolished. Bismarck did more than acquiesce. Much of the liberalizing legislation was passed by the Customs Parliament, even before the creation of the Empire, under the guidance of Germany's leading advocate of free trade, Rudolf von Delbrück, whom he appointed as Secretary of the Chancellery in 1867. He freely gave the middle class these economic concessions, so that he would not have to offer the constitutional ones that were the Progressives' *raison d'être* and that still retained a place even in the National Liberals' programme.

The second link in the alliance between Bismarck and the Liberals was the matter of Church–state relations. In one sense Germany was simply experiencing the anti-clerical offensive familiar in Italy and Spain, France and Belgium, Switzerland and Austria. The Catholic Church had isolated itself intellectually with the 1864 Syllabus of Errors, with its denunciations of Liberalism, secularism, and rationalism. The 1870 Declaration of Papal Infallibility further provoked its enemies and embarrassed many of its friends. The implication in the declaration that the spiritual power had authority over the secular threatened the sovereignty of the new German state and sought to undermine the patriotism and loyalty of one-third of its citizens. However, the matter became troublesome to the Government only through the split in the German Catholic Church which resulted from the declaration, and the emergence of an anti-infallibilist group, the Old Catholics, led by two eminent lay scholars, Ignaz Döllinger and Johann Friedrich.

Initially it was a Prussian problem. The arrangement in force since 1840 had given both Protestant and Catholic Churches considerable internal freedom as well as a state subsidy. After the Old Catholic split, there was increasing evidence of victimization of dissident teachers, paid by the taxpayer but appointed by the Church. These isolated incidents brought out the latent hostility between the Church and Zentrum on the one hand, of Bismarck and the Liberals on the other. The Zentrum's attachment to the old, federal Greater German order turned them, in Bismarck's eyes, into *Reichsfeinde* (enemies of the Empire), in the Liberals' eyes into traitors to the national idea. The Church, on the other hand, saw its worst fears of impending aggression by the state confirmed, fears which had been the *raison d'être* for the formation of the Zentrum.

Just as Bismarck pushed through the liberalization of the German economy by appointing a dedicated Liberal, Delbrück, to supervise it, so he turned to an ideologically reliable official in his fight with the Church, and made Adalbert Falk Prussian Minister of Religious Affairs in 1872. The 1840 compromise had evidently ceased to be workable. For Falk the supremacy of state over Church was an article of faith: 'should the state Government not be capable of countering the conflagration of the Church conflict with effective energy, then the extensive intervention of the legislature will become necessary', he wrote in one of his earliest memoranda to the Prussian Government.

And indeed appropriate legislation was not lacking. It began with laws giving the state the right to inspect schools and banning the Jesuit order from Prussia. It reached its climax with the so-called May laws of May 1873. These gave the state power over the education of priests, and removed many of the disciplinary powers of bishops. In the years that followed civil marriage was made compulsory, all religious orders except medical ones dissolved, and the constitutional guarantees of self-government to the churches rescinded.

Bismarck was an orthodox Lutheran; believing in the 'priesthood of all believers', he was naturally out of sympathy with the claims of Rome and the Catholic hierarchy. But his primary quarrel was not with the Church as an institution: it was with the *Reichsfeinde* who preached disloyalty, whether in parliament or from the pulpit, who persisted in Polish-language teaching in the eastern provinces, who encouraged autonomist sentiments in newly annexed Alsace and Lorraine, who urged military intervention against Germany's ally,

Italy, to liberate the Pope, and who sought the sympathy of the right-wing, revanchist Government in France.

While these diplomatic considerations also appealed to the parliamentary Liberals, the ideological impulse of the conflict mattered most to them. The mantle of Voltaire seemed to have fallen on their shoulders. It was the Progressive intellectual Virchow who declared that the contest 'daily acquires more of the character of the great cultural conflict of the human race'. The *Kulturkampf*, as it came to be known, had profound and lasting effects on German public life. It gave German Catholicism the halo of martyrdom. The policy of passive resistance enjoined by the hierarchy led many priests, including two archbishops, to prison. Above all it strengthened the zeal of the laity. In the 1874 Reichstag elections the Zentrum vote doubled and the Liberals' hopes of a secure base in the economically advanced and intellectually open region of the Rhineland—one of the strongholds of radicalism in 1848—were dashed. German Catholicism was confirmed as a minority culture, at one remove from the mainstream of national life—inward-looking, often backward-looking. German Catholics remained poorer, worse educated, and under-represented in the public service compared with their fellow citizens. There were virtually no Catholics in the highest ranks of business or finance. In the 1880s a Protestant boy stood twice as good a chance of going to university as a Catholic; as late as 1924, only 12 per cent of the highest-ranking civil servants were Catholics. These inequalities have not been entirely eliminated even in the second half of the twentieth century.

A rather more short-term consequence of the severity of the *Kulturkampf* was its effect on the Prussian Conservatives and the royal family. Many of the Junker class had strong anti-Catholic prejudices. But unlike the Liberals they did not care for the secularizing implications of the *Kulturkampf* and they had a powerful ally in the Empress Augusta, who exerted strong influence on her husband in ecclesiastical matters. The Catholic Church was, in the last resort, a bulwark against paganism and materialism: when Wilhelm I declared that 'religion must be preserved for the people', he did not distinguish between denominations. The more his own class and the court were alienated from him, the more Bismarck had to lean on the Liberal Reichstag majority. The more dependent he was on them, the harder they might press for greater parliamentary powers. He had therefore to find a way of restoring relations with the Conservatives and, if possible, the Zentrum. He found it in economic policy.

The boom which had gathered pace in the 1860s continued into the 1870s. Germany, which in 1840 had lagged behind France and even Belgium in iron, steel, and textile production, was now the leading industrial power on the continent. The boom came to only a temporary halt with a bank crash in 1873; the psychological and political consequences of this crash were, however, profound. The idea of unfettered economic competition, of relying solely on the forces of supply and demand to bring prosperity and happiness, was both new and unpopular in Germany. The doctrines of what Disraeli had dubbed 'the school of Manchester' tended to atomize and subvert society. Conservatives disliked this because they were emotionally tied to a society based on land, crafts, and hierarchy; but so did many Liberals because they saw individualism as the enemy of strong national feeling.

In the 1840s the economist Friedrich List had advocated protective tariffs and self-sufficiency for political as well as economic reasons—free trade was fit for philistine foreigners: Englishmen, Jews, and the like. Connected with this attitude was a paternalistic social conscience, supported by both the bureaucracy and academic opinion. Thus Prussia, though hardly yet industrialized, prohibited factory labour for children under twelve in 1853, well in advance of any such measure in Britain. In 1872, when the boom was still unchecked, a group of Germany's leading economists and lawyers, including Gustav Schmoller, Lujo Brentano, and Rudolf Gneist, founded the Verein für Sozialpolitik (Association for Social Policy), to advocate 'well-considered intervention by the state for the protection of the justified interests of all participants'. This group, nicknamed *Kathedersozialisten* ('professorial Socialists'), differed sharply from the proletarian Socialists. They were neither democrats nor egalitarians. But in the short run they were more influential—with the Churches, with some of the aristocracy, at the court, and with Bismarck. They demonstrated how foreign the ethos of cut-throat business competition was to the culture of Germany—foreign, one might say, until domesticated by Ludwig Erhard and the post-1948 'economic miracle'. They demonstrated what a temporary, though remarkable, deviation the speculation mania of 1867–73 was, that promoters' era, the *Gründerzeit*, whose name was soon to become an evil memory and term of abuse.

The chief impetus towards a new economic policy, however, was the crash of 1873, for it undermined the confidence of the entrepreneurs. They were disturbed by falling prices, by British competition, by the unrest that might follow unemployment. The conservatively inclined magnates of heavy industry, men like Carl Freiherr von Stumm and Wilhelm von Kardorff of the Reichspartei, became the chief spokesmen of the Centralverein Deutscher Industrieller (CDI), the first really effective industrial pressure group. However, 'industry' or 'business' are not homogeneous interests that can speak with a uniform voice. There remained plenty of businessmen who did not like the new body and who, out of Liberal principle, did not care for the proposed link with the state. To make sure of success, therefore, the protectionist lobby needed an ally. It found one in agriculture.

Farmers in general, and the big landlords in the east in particular, had felt pushed to one side during the rush to favour industry and commerce. Quick profits seemed to be honoured more than slow cultivation. But as long as Germany was a net exporter of grain, they had nothing to gain from protective tariffs. By 1876, under the pressure of urbanization, Germany was a net importer of wheat; and this change coincided with the flooding of Europe with cheap, high-grade prairie wheat following the completion of North American transcontinental railways. So, by 1876, the first agricultural protection society was founded to propagate 'ideas and principles of a mutually beneficial economy, resting on Christian principles'. The association's leaders were, overwhelmingly, large landowners from the East, although 80 per cent of Germany's farms belonged to peasants with family holdings. These peasants, mainly in the West and South, many of them dependent on cheap fodder for the poultry-, pig-, and dairy-farming that was more profitable for them, had to be persuaded to make common cause with the Junkers. This was not too difficult. The small farmers had hitherto lacked political leadership; their resentments against towns, commerce, and organized labour could easily be exploited, with a plentiful dose of the anti-Semitism that formed an integral part of agrarian propaganda.

A united conservative front of industry and agriculture was, therefore, not easy to bring about. Each wing had to deal with dissidents in its own ranks and their demands were not all that compatible: manufacturers did not love dear bread and farmers did not love dear machines. But it could agree on a minimum programme. It could demand the head of Delbrück, and Bismarck, who was anxious to keep his options open, obliged. That the alliance would, within three years, secure all its essential demands was not, at this stage, to be foreseen. It was to come about through a conjunction of domestic and diplomatic, social and religious, economic and constitutional considerations; it was to have effects on the evolution of the Empire far beyond the fiscal merits of this or that import duty.

Of the non-economic factors, three favoured the protectionists. The first was Bismarck's desire to reduce the political influence of the National Liberals. He first tried to achieve this by inviting the National Liberal leader, Bennigsen, whom he regarded as a moderate, into the Prussian cabinet; he might hope thereby to tempt Bennigsen into a less independent line. But Bennigsen refused to enter except as a party leader and in company with two party colleagues. That was in December 1877. The negotiations were never completed because two months later Pope Pius IX died. Pius IX had been an ardent supporter of the Zentrum, refusing all requests to act as a mediator. As long as he lived any retreat from the *Kulturkampf* was all but impossible, and as long as the *Kulturkampf* lasted the National Liberals were indispensable. Now, with the election of a more conciliatory Leo XIII as Pope, a choice was possible.

In May and June there followed two attempts on the life of the Emperor, the first by a subnormal adolescent, the second, which injured Wilhelm quite seriously, by an anarchist, Dr Karl Nobiling. The genuine public indignation which followed these acts of violence gave Bismarck a heaven-sent opportunity. After the Reichstag had turned down an ill-drafted bill to ban the Social Democratic Party, which was blamed—without evidence—for the assassination attempts, he dissolved the Reichstag although it was only a year since elections had taken place. Out of the electoral campaign, which was conducted against *Umsturz* (subversion) and in favour of *Ordnung* (order), there emerged a majority which from Bismarck's point of view was conservative, from the protectionists' point of view pro-tariff. Bismarck was no doubt genuinely frightened by the growth of Social Democracy and especially by the party's gains in 1877—it was, after all, only a few years since the Paris Commune, which had been publicly acclaimed by August Bebel. But he also saw clearly that an illiberal proposal like this would embarrass and possibly split the National Liberals, for ever divided between patriotism and civil liberties. As for tariffs, Bismarck saw no particular virtue in them—he was, in matters of economic policy, an agnostic—and he did not cherish feather-bedding heavy industry. But he had a sincere emotional link with the land and could see the advantages of strengthening that conservative interest.

The Conservative Phase

After the elections, the Conservative parties, for the first time since 1871, had almost as many deputies as the Liberal parties. The anti-Socialist law, which forbade Socialist meetings, gave the police arbitrary powers of search, arrest, and banishment and even empowered the Government to declare a state of siege, was quickly passed with the shamefaced assent of the National Liberals. The Zentrum voted against. They recognized another outsider when they saw one; they could not very well complain of discrimination and yet tolerate it against others. The anti-Socialist law, like the *Kulturkampf* measure, showed that the principle of equality before the law was not sacrosanct under the Empire and that a democratically elected parliament was not a secure defence against breaches of that principle. Indeed it showed that, suitably manipulated, parliamentary majorities could give such discrimination a legitimacy that it would otherwise have lacked. In the long run the discrimination was counter-productive. Official persecution, though it temporarily harmed the Socialists' electoral effort, merely strengthened their cohesion and determination. It also widened the gulf between themselves and the rest of society, and thus had the same effect on them as the *Kulturkampf* on the Catholics. The

common experience of persecution also led to a curious political cama-
raderie between Socialists and Catholics, unbridgeable though the
ideological gulf might seem. Their mass bases gave them resources
which the other parties lacked; they alone survived the political holocaust of 1918 intact and co-operated not only in founding but in
governing the Weimar Republic. From 1919 to 1932 they headed, in
coalition, the now-democratized Government of Prussia.

Having refused to follow Bismarck in persecuting the Labour
movement, the Zentrum now prepared to join him on the tariff question. They favoured tariffs intrinsically, because they represented, in
the main, economically vulnerable classes, but also because their social
theory favoured state regulation of private competition. Above all,
however, they saw tariff reform as a way of ending the *Kulturkampf*,
indeed as a way of becoming part of the governmental majority.

The tariff bill was passed in 1879. It was a 'package', giving
concessions to both industrialists and landowners. The National Liberals were divided on the first and opposed to the second. But what
emphasized the ever-widening gulf between Bismarck and them was
that the bulk of the new revenue was to go not to the Imperial treasury
but to the individual states. This accorded with the federalist tenets of
the Zentrum; it accorded with Bismarck's desire to raise taxes without
parliamentary interference; it ran directly counter to any Liberal doctrine that parliament must remain sovereign over an annual budget.

The tariff debate was the last straw for the left wing of
the National Liberal Party. Led by Eduard Lasker and Ludwig
Bamberger they seceded in 1880 and later joined with the Progressive
Party in a new Left-Liberal body, the Deutschfreisinnige Partei. What
remained of the National Liberals was a chauvinistic rump. In 1881
they held only 47 seats; seven years earlier it had been 155. The
Bennigsen episode was unlikely to be repeated. In contrast, Bismarck
had to be more respectful to the wishes of the Zentrum. Falk was
dismissed from his ministry, but the *Kulturkampf* laws were dismantled only slowly and never completely. Nevertheless, German
politics had taken a crucial change of direction.

The protection campaign had never restricted itself to purely
fiscal objectives. It was anti-Liberal in every sense. Its spokesmen
emphasized that they were out to break 'the essential achievements of

the year 1848 . . . We shall have to return to the so-called patrimonial and patriarchal state'. They wanted 'economic legislation that will reawaken the people's feeling for authority'. There is no doubt that the success of their agitation reversed the direction of German politics. The virtual disintegration of the National Liberal Party marked the end of the crucial alliance between Bismarck and German Liberalism in creating the Empire. Though the National Liberals made great concessions of principle—excessive concessions in the eyes of many— to secure the united Germany they desired, the Empire that emerged would have been less liberal without their collaboration. For the best part of the decade Bismarck needed them as much as they needed him. While they could never dominate German politics without him, the moment Bismarck decided that he could govern without them, their key role was under threat. Bismarck had, as we have seen, many motives for the change of course. Not the least of them was the fear that the ageing Emperor would be succeeded by his son Friedrich, married to a daughter of Queen Victoria, who shared his Liberal sympathies.

The change of course meant that the prospect of genuine parliamentary government in Germany became quite remote. Bismarck relieved himself of the prospect of control not only by the Liberal majority, but by a majority formed by any one party on the Westminster model. Whether this was ever a strong threat must remain an open question. Not even in the southern states, where parliaments had a longer history, did any class have much experience of self-government; less still in Prussia. German parliamentarians were often learned debaters, sometimes skilled negotiators, but they were not statesmen. Bismarck repeatedly taunted them with being skilled only at opposition: if the Government were to call their bluff and resign, they could not possibly form a ministry. The National Liberal historian Heinrich von Sybel, writing in the London *Fortnightly Review*, explained the difference between British and German parliamentary conventions thus.

No-one in England would understand an Opposition which attacked a Ministry without wishing to occupy its place . . .
Even now the majority of electors regard the criticism and control of the

Government as the most important part of a member's duty . . . A candidate who allowed it to be seen that he possessed both the power and the wish to become a minister would immediately forfeit the support of a large number of the constituencies. . . .

When, in the year 1863, the Liberal Minister in Baden, Baron Roggenbach, sent in his resignation (in consequence of the rejection of an important Bill by a Liberal Chamber), and called on the Grand Duke to summon the leader of the Opposition to the Cabinet, the victorious party declared that they would submit to no such *unheard-of violence*, that it was the duty of Roggenbach to retain office, but to suit himself to the duties and wishes of the representative body. The English reader will see at once, that while the majority entertain sentiments like these, parliamentary government is not to be thought of, that it is impossible, in the midst of these parliamentary parties to form a school of practical statesmen.

A fragmented parliament, whose members spoke for rival interest groups, was much more convenient to Bismarck, and after 1879 the already strong trend in this direction was accelerated. Because political parties were excluded—and, as we have seen, chose to be excluded— from the responsibilities of office, their behaviour tended to be irresponsible and their electoral campaigns demagogic. Because of this tendency to irresponsibility and demagogy it was easy for the opponents of parliamentarization to claim that German party politicians were unfit to govern. The agitational role of the parties led to a change in the type of person attracted to politics. The sociologist Max Weber has distinguished those politicians who live 'für die Politik' ('for politics') from those who live 'von der Politik' ('off politics'). The notables who still predominated in the 1870s gave way to the professional politicians: professional not in the sense that belonging to the Reichstag was a full-time occupation—its sessions were short and members were unpaid until 1906—but in the sense that they were the salaried employees of party machines or economic lobbies. By 1912 nearly one member in four was a professional of this type.

With the decline of the National Liberal Party, and the withdrawal of its most distinguished leaders into opposition, the social and political ideals of the protectionists now became those of the Government. The victorious alliance was not so much one of 'industry' and 'agriculture'—these categories were altogether too diverse inter nally—but of iron and rye. Thus the most traditionalist and paternalist sections of Germany's economic leaders became the most influential, and remained so until 1918. Therein lies the real significance of the tariff of 1879.

Its most immediate effects were to be seen in the reorganization of the civil service and the army. The lower ranks of the Prussian civil service were largely staffed by former army regulars, the provincial administrations headed by aristocrats. It was these two types of official who helped to give German bureaucrats their reputation for arrogance and pedantry. But the middle and higher ranks, both in Berlin and the provinces, were largely recruited from the liberal-minded bourgeoisie, deistic and enlightened, and had been so ever since the reforms of Freiherr vom Stein at the beginning of the century. Of the National Liberal deputies in 1874, fifty-one—almost a third—were professional civil servants. In Germany, and indeed most of continental Europe, in contrast with Britain and the United States, there is no incompatibility between elective office and a civil service post.

Though the Prussian civil service and judiciary could not be purged, they could be disciplined. As those officials recruited or promoted in the Liberal decades reached retirement, they were replaced with more pliable men. A royal decree of 4 December 1882 reminded all civil servants that they were the King's subordinates and required to support his and his ministers' policies. By the mid-1880s it was possible to ban the actor Bernays from the royal theatres because he had addressed an 'oppositional' (i.e. Liberal) meeting; by the mid-1890s the reintegration of the bureaucracy into the values and outlook of pre-liberal Prussia caused Prince Hohenlohe-Schillingfürst, the Chancellor, to record:

When I sit among the Prussian excellencies, the contrast between North and South Germany becomes clear to me . . . The Germans are right when they see my presence in Berlin as a guarantee of national unity . . . I have to endeavour here to keep Prussia attached to the *Reich*, for all these gentlemen do not give a fig for the *Reich* and would sooner be rid of it today than tomorrow.

The consequence of this was that though Prussians did not monopolize the new Imperial civil service, they could command its ethos.

Non-Prussians who were suspected of Liberalism or particularism found entry difficult. It is this that accounts for the sparsity of Catholics, and for the almost total absence of—at any rate unbaptized—Jews. In theory the civil service stood above party and served only the state. But since loyalty to the state was measured in largely partisan terms, this fiction became less and less easy to maintain.

The same pressures towards social and political conformity were felt in the army, for even the army had its battle with the civilian spirit. Indeed, it was the proposal to disband the *Landwehr*, the civilian militia dating from the Wars of Liberation, that had sparked off the constitutional conflict of the 1860s. Much more than the civil service, the army had always reflected the rural social structure of eastern Prussia: the landowner commanded, the peasant obeyed. To the maintenance of this order the *Landwehr* had always seemed an irrelevance and a disruption. As late as 1913 half the army officers above the rank of colonel were aristocrats. Similarly some regiments, especially in the guards and the cavalry, remained almost entirely aristocratic. Nevertheless, as the army expanded and as technical complexity demanded higher educational requirements, a gradual *embourgeoisement* did take place. This happened particularly through the institution of the reserve officer, which was to replace the *Landwehr*. Many deplored this dilution. Count Alfred von Waldersee, who succeeded the elder Moltke as Chief of Staff, noted that

many old and even active officers decide on a different career for their sons. Sons of petty officials, shopkeepers, and so on will soon form the majority of the new infantry officers, the sons of *nouveau riche* industrialists push themselves into the cavalry and ruin the still simple way of life.

But there were advantages in the new arrangement, too. It was a way of binding the middle class, especially the socially ambitious, to the most conservative institution in the state, an idea popularized for instance in Franz Adam Bayerlein's novel *Jena oder Sedan*. Moreover, since a reserve officer had to be acceptable to his regiment, his rank held more prestige than in the old *Landwehr* (which was raised by the municipality), and the social and political selection could be more stringent. A reserve officer, like a regular officer, was subject to regimental *Ehrengerichte* (courts of honour), and liable to fight duels, contrary though these might be to the civil legal code. A Jew was no more eligible for a reserve than a regular commission. A Social Democrat, too, lacked the 'moral qualities' (according to the Ministry of War, a bare six months before the outbreak of the First World War) even for the one-year *Einjahr-Freiwilligen* service—the special concession for the academically qualified. Liberals, too, might suffer: more than one scion of a distinguished family was asked to resign his reserve commission for voting the wrong way in parliament. But for every non-conformist who was victimized, there were ten who liked playing soldiers and were delighted with the entrée that their uniform gave into Old Prussian society. It was a further aspect, inseparable from the others, of the integration of the urban middle class into an order based on land and patriarchal authority. The Government's aim in this policy was twofold: to disarm potential Liberals by offering them social privileges while at the same time, as we have seen, removing the last vestiges of parliamentary control over personnel matters.

The impulses towards greater national and social solidarity were not exclusively repressive. There were two main reasons for this. The anti-Socialist law—'the Law for Combating the Criminal Aims of Social Democracy', to give it its full title—was based on genuine fear of revolution and for the remainder of the Empire's lifetime there were constant rumours of *coups d'état* or of threats to suspend parliament, though none of these came to anything. But Bismarck and his advisers were aware that the growth of Social Democracy stemmed from genuine grievances. This realization encouraged the Government to call on the old German tradition of seeing a positive role for the state, in particular in regulating social and economic relations. The social welfare measures—'practical Christianity', according to the Emperor—passed between 1883 and 1889 were intended to win workers back to piety and loyalty. Building on a patchwork of existing schemes they created a system of sickness and accident insurance (with the premiums of the latter paid by employers only) and old-age pensions. They were gradually extended to cover dependants, too. By 1914 some 16 million persons were insured against sickness and old age and some 28 million against industrial accidents. Germany was the world's most advanced Welfare State. The agitation of the Verein für Sozialpolitik was crowned with success, in a way which would not have happened had the *laissez-faire* Liberals continued to dominate the Reichstag. Explaining the absence of revolutionary sentiment in Britain in the 1850s, the German writer Theodor Fontane observed that though 'the state does nothing *for* the people, neither does it do anything *against* them'. In Germany the state could at times be highly oppressive, but it could also be effectively paternalistic.

The new domestic policy and the new balance of social forces saw a revival of illiberal ways of thought not merely in the narrowly political sphere but in the intellectual climate of the country. The career of Heinrich von Treitschke illustrates this. He had, in the 1860s, been a leading member of the Nationalverein and a leading opponent of Prussian absolutism—partly, but not solely, because he thought the Hohenzollerns would be both unwilling and unable to bring about national unification. Like many Liberals he made his peace with Bismarck; unlike some of these, he drifted into increasingly conservative, authoritarian, and intolerant attitudes. As he did so, his audience, academic and lay, grew.

In 1873 he was appointed Professor of History at Berlin. In 1874 he began his series of lectures on *Politik*, which were for many students their chief introduction to the subject and which were filled with superficial and tasteless remarks about German and non-German national character. In 1879 he published the first volume of his *Deutsche Geschichte im 19. Jahrhundert*, a paean to a Prussia predestined to lead Germany. But he achieved more immediate impact with a series of articles in *Preußische Jahrbücher*, of which he was now editor, in which he emphasized the Christian character of the German state and railed against Jewish influence and especially Jewish immigration (whose extent he greatly exaggerated):

Year after year there pours across our eastern frontier . . . from the inexhaustible Polish cradle, a host of ambitious trouser-selling youths, whose children and children's children are one day to dominate Germany's stock exchanges and newspapers . . . Right into the most educated circles . . . we can hear, as if from one mouth, 'The Jews are our misfortune'.

Ever since the bank crash of 1873 there had been voices blaming the Jews for the evils of the day, but they remained largely unheard.

'What *he* said . . . was thereby made respectable', the historian Harry Breßlau wrote to Theodor Mommsen. Treitschke's outburst coincided with the political campaign of one of the court chaplains, Adolf Stöcker, who, appalled at the growing secularization of life in the capital and alarmed at the progress of Social Democracy, tried to found a Christian-Social Workers' Party to convert the working class to monarchism and the middle class to social welfare. The working-class audience at which he aimed took no notice of him, but clerks and shopkeepers did respond to his anti-Liberal tirades, and Stöcker soon spiced these with anti-Semitic slogans.

Treitschke's articles and Stöcker's speeches had a particular effect on student opinion. In 1881 delegates sympathetic to the new cause met on the Kyffhäuser mountain and founded the Verein deutscher Studenten, the first and most important right-wing student organization for many decades. Max Weber, a student at Berlin in the 1880s, complained of the 'frenetic cheers' which greeted any anti-Semitic remark by Treitschke and the widespread anti-Semitic graffiti 'of varying coarseness'. 'The most incredible thing, however,' he wrote to Hermann Baumgarten, 'is the fantastic ignorance of the history of this century among my contemporaries . . . apart from a few crimes by the Left and Bismarck's achievements. Inside their heads domestic politics began in 1878'.

The reaction against liberal principles at the end of the 1870s had many causes—humanitarian, aesthetic, and religious. There was a widespread fear that Liberalism would lead to moral decay and political subversion. Underlying all these, there was a desire to find a meaning in the new nation-state which went deeper than administrative formulae and paragraphs on trade; the hope that the sacrifices and victories of the 1860s would lead to a new golden age of German prestige and influence; above all, the determination that no power, military or ideological, should threaten the newly achieved. In Germany, lacking natural frontiers and surrounded by long-established but wary powers, considerations of foreign policy could never be ignored during the domestic debate—certainly not by Bismarck, whether the subject was the *Kulturkampf* or tariffs. Germany was now a power; most of her influential citizens wanted her to be a *Machstaat*. It was a new situation for Europe.

Germany and the World

Few contemporaries missed the significance of the victory of Prussia over France in 1870. 'Europe has lost a mistress and gained a master' was a widely heard verdict. The harshness of the peace terms imposed on France—the annexation of Alsace and Lorraine and an indemnity of five million gold francs—confirmed many fears that Europe was not at the end but at the beginning of a period of Prussian expansion. There were many witnesses to the bellicose, arrogant public mood of Germany in the wake of these victories. 'Oh, how the poor German nation will be deceived', wrote the Swiss historian Jacob Burckhardt to his friend Friedrich Preen, 'if it wants to stand the rifle in the corner at home, and give itself over to the arts and fortunes of peace! The call will be: carry on drilling!', and Friedrich Nietzsche, appalled at the popular notion that German military superiority somehow implied German cultural superiority, warned that 'A great victory is a great danger'; it risked 'the defeat, even the extirpation, of the German spirit in favour of the "German *Reich*"'.

Certainly Bismarck's successes had given the German public, and many men in high places, a taste for national self-assertion and quick, violent solutions. Bismarck himself did not share these predilections even though his 'iron and blood' rhetoric encouraged them. He had been concerned to secure the hegemony of Prussia in Central Europe and to this end he needed to displace, but not destroy, Austria, to reduce the power of France, and to keep the goodwill of Russia. After 1871 he was concerned to maintain these achievements, with all the conservatism of the successful revolutionary, but the means to this end was now peace, not war. Threats to the Bismarckian order could come from two sources. The first was a desire for revenge by France, and for this reason he needed to keep France diplomatically isolated. In the first few years this was difficult. France had a right-wing, royalist government, well connected internationally; to break these connections was one of the purposes of the *Kulturkampf*. After 1877, when the republican ascendancy began in France, he needed to bother less about this danger. The other threat came from the Balkans where, ever since the Crimean War, Austria had been trying to sustain the decaying Turkish Empire while Russia tended to support the Turks' subject nationalities—mostly Christian and predominantly Slav—in the hope of furthering her own expansion towards Constantinople and the Mediterranean.

To keep the rival empires at peace Bismarck encouraged the formation, in 1872–3, of the Three Emperors' League, ostensibly with the common purpose of maintaining the monarchical political order. This was not entirely a smokescreen. The revolutions of 1848 had been a frightening experience, the Paris Commune of 1871 even more so. The First Working Men's International, founded by Marx in 1864, never amounted to very much, divided as it was by sectarian quarrels; but this is more obvious today than it was at the time. Even so, the main purpose of the Emperors' League was diplomatic, and in this it failed. Within a few years it was tested by both of the kinds of crisis that menaced Germany most, and found wanting.

The first test came from France. The speed of French economic recovery after the defeat worried Germany; the beginnings of military recovery even more. In 1875 Bismarck instigated a number of anti-French press articles, the most alarmist of which bore the headline 'War in sight?' The effect of this was to rouse both Russia and Britain. Both states were convinced that a new Franco–German war would further weaken France, both feared that such an outcome would give Germany an intolerable preponderance in Europe. Both therefore warned Bismarck of their alarm. This co-operation by Russia and Britain on behalf of France was ominous. It was a premonition of 1914. It lent substance to that 'nightmare of alliances'—*le cauchemar des coalitions*—from which Bismarck freely admitted that he suffered. It illustrated how easily Germany might have to face enemies on two fronts and how Germans might be tempted to interpret as 'encirclement' a situation which others saw as a reasonable counterweight to German hegemonial designs.

The second crisis involved the Balkans. Its immediate causes were revolts by Bulgarians and Bosnian Serbs against Turkish rule. Bismarck very much hoped to stay out of this quarrel; it involved no interests. But he could not stay out, for the interests of his allies were irreconcilable. Austria was determined to maintain the integrity of the Turkish Empire, partly to block Russia, partly because the triumph of national self-determination would necessarily undermine the multinational structure of the Habsburg monarchy. Russian policy was more ambiguous. There was a conservative faction which favoured good relations with Germany and therefore an unadventurous foreign policy. But there was also an increasingly powerful pan-Slav faction which favoured a course of intervention and liberation, and the more desperate the situation of the Balkan Slavs became in 1876–7, the more they had the ear of the Tsar. Accordingly, Russia declared war on, and defeated, Turkey. The peace, signed at San Stefano, was dictated by the Russian ambassador at Constantinople, Count Ignatiev, an extreme pan-Slav: it drastically reduced Turkish rule in Europe, created a large independent Bulgarian state with an outlet to the Aegean, and omitted any compensation for Austria. This was not only contrary to a secret agreement between the Russian and Austrian Governments, it was offensive to the rest of Europe because it marked a serious shift in the balance of power. The new Bulgaria was seen as a potential satellite of Russia and to Disraeli, the British Prime Minister, as a particular threat to Britain's route to India.

Only a European conference could settle these conflicts; the statesman most interested in preventing the other powers from coming to blows—or from forming an alliance which he could not control—but least interested in the geographical details was Bismarck. So the congress met in Berlin in 1878 under his presidency and this was in itself significant. The last conference to discuss the Near East had been held in Paris in 1856, after the Crimean War of 1854–5. The Congress of Berlin could have only one outcome: to secure from Russia some disgorging of the gains of San Stefano. In addition Austria gained the right to occupy the former Turkish provinces of Bosnia and Herzegovina. Much as Bismarck tried to hold the balance between Russia and her antagonists, Russia inevitably saw him as an opponent and Austria as an ally. The new relationships seemed to be confirmed when the Dual Alliance was signed the next year between Austria and Germany. Though the terms were defensive (and secret), and though Bismarck saw it as much as a restraint on Austria as moral support for anti-Russian adventures, it demonstrated that Germany's fate was in the last resort more strongly tied to Austria. Bismarck himself had spelt this out to the Russians in 1876:

Our first requirement is to maintain friendship among the great monarchies . . . If, to our regret, this should not be possible between Russia and Austria, then we could tolerate our friends' losing or winning battles against each other, but not that one of them should be so severely injured or damaged as to endanger its status as an independent Great Power, with a voice in Europe.

It was Austria rather than Russia for whom he feared such an extreme fate. It was to be avoided not only for balance-of-power reasons, but because the collapse of the Habsburg monarchy would reopen all those questions of Greater or Lesser Germany which he hoped had been settled once and for all in 1871.

The year 1879 was the beginning of the special relationship between Germany and Austria, which lasted until 1918 and in which the weaker partner was increasingly able to blackmail the stronger. However, though Austria was from now on Germany's one reliable ally, this was not the situation Bismarck desired. He wanted reconciliation with Russia, though his agricultural tariffs made this even more difficult; he wanted to bring in Britain to bolster Austria's defences in the Balkans; he wanted to include Italy—a potential enemy of Austria and a potential friend of France—in his system. He wanted to ensure that Germany would always be 'à trois in a Europe of five', and that he himself would remain, in the words of the French ambassador, 'arbitre suprême des destinées des trois Empires'.

Initially he seemed highly successful in mending the broken fences. In 1881 the Three Emperors' League was revived, Russia having decided that isolation did not benefit her. In 1882 Italy joined Austria and Germany, making the Dual a Triple Alliance, in return for help in her colonial and naval ambitions in the Mediterranean. But the new structure was fragile. France could not be kept permanently from reasserting herself. Bismarck had encouraged her in colonial adventures as a distraction, but when these failed, nationalist passions were diverted towards Europe again, fanned by a flamboyant, politically ambitious general, Georges Boulanger, who was made minister for War in 1886 and who embarked on an electoral campaign devoted to 'revanche'.

For a time there was a distinct risk of war in the West. More significant, however, was the echo which Boulangism found in Russia. Pan-Slavism prospered in the 1880s. Alexander III, who became Tsar in 1881 and who was more autocratic and reactionary than his assassinated father, had some sympathy with the notion that Slavs had special spiritual and moral qualities that set them aside from others—especially from Teutons—and that Russia had a divinely appointed mission to lead the other Slav peoples. And many influential Russians continued to feel that Bismarck's behaviour at Berlin had been poor recompense for Russia's benevolence during his own wars against Austria and France. In Paris the crowds sang

> Avec le Tsar, pour Dieu, France, pour la patrie,
> Mort aux Prussiens, et vive Boulanger

and the pan-Slav press reciprocated with eulogies of France. It was unlikely that the Tsar would base his diplomacy on an unstable adventurer like Boulanger, who indeed disappeared from the scene in 1889, but the ice had been broken.

In 1887, Russia refused to renew the Three Emperors' League and secured instead the bilateral agreement known as the Reinsurance Treaty, whose secret clauses bound Germany to stronger support of Russia than the merely defensive agreement of 1881. This promise was inconsistent with those to Austria in the Dual and Triple Alliances; it was inconsistent also with the terms of the 'Mediterranean Entente' which Bismarck now fathered, under the terms of which Italy and (at last) Britain were to help Austria in preventing Russian expansion. Bismarck was apparently determined to maintain at all costs the two cardinal principles of his foreign policy: to retain the friendship of Russia, and to ensure the survival of Austria. But the most immediate tangible benefit to him was in domestic politics. The bellicose noises of Boulanger and the coquetry of Russia ensured a tame parliamentary majority in the 1887 Reichstag election—the so-called *Kartell* of the National Liberals and the two Conservative parties—which passed the septennial military budget without any fuss.

Whether these complex diplomatic schemes and the uncannily quiet domestic climate had any real chances of long-term survival was never put to the test. In 1888 the old Emperor died; within ninety-nine days his son, Friedrich III, already suffering from cancer when he ascended the throne, was also dead. The new Emperor was Wilhelm's grandson, Wilhelm II. He was twenty-nine years old, a representative of a new generation which took Bismarck's achievements—German unity, and Germany's place as a power—for granted and was impatient for greater things. Bismarck had been born in 1815, the year of the Congress of Vienna; Wilhelm II in 1859, three years before Bismarck became Prime Minister of Prussia. Their worlds were far apart.

Twenty years of Bismarckian policy management showed both how much had changed and how little. The German Empire was now a major power; it could not dictate, but it could not be ignored. Yet one conundrum, left over from before 1871, remained unanswered: was the German Question a domestic one or a diplomatic one? Again and again domestic and foreign politics overlapped. The Austro-Hungarian Empire needed to be preserved so as not to reopen the old conflict between a Lesser and a Greater Germany. Above all, both foreign policy considerations and the social conservatism of Prussia's rulers kept another old question alive: who was to control the army? The 1883 promotion of the Prussian Military Cabinet kept parliamentary intruders at bay. The victory of the *Kartell* parties in the Reichstag election of 1887, ensuring the 10 per cent increase in the strength of the army, showed that Bismarck had not lost the knack of manipulating public opinion, or that of turning a diplomatic crisis to domestic advantage.

3 The Wilhelmine Empire, 1890–1914

> The German Empire has been built more truly on coal and iron than on blood and iron.
>
> (John Maynard Keynes, *The Economic Consequences of the Peace*, 1919)

Economy and Society

It became a cliché in the 1960s that while Germany had become an economic giant she remained a political dwarf. The observation could have been applied as well to the 1890s. The outsider, viewing Bismarck's diplomatic and military successes over the previous thirty years, might think that Germany had done very well for herself. In Germany itself, there was a growing feeling that too little had been achieved; that the Empire was still a power of medium rank rather than of true world status; that Germany's influence in the world was not keeping pace with her economic expansion.

Maynard Keynes was not alone in pointing to the economic roots of German power. Not only would Bismarck have found it much more difficult to win over middle-class opinion and the southern states without the Prussian economic dynamism of the 1860s, but industry, and especially heavy industry, forged ahead from 1867 onwards, profiting from political unity and only briefly impeded by the banking crash of 1873. It was therefore a stimulant as well as a sustainer of both entrepreneurial self-interest and national self-confidence. The figures alone show how decisively Germany had seized the economic leadership of Europe by the time of the First World War.

Between 1870 and 1913 the productive capacity of Germany increased eightfold, while that of Britain doubled and that of France tripled. Only the United States, among major producers, showed a faster rate of growth. By 1893 German steel production had overtaken

British; by 1910 Germany's iron and steel exports exceeded Britain's. The metallurgical hegemony of Britain, already dented by America, was further reduced. But the figures alone tell only half the story. The German economy in 1870, though prosperous and expanding, had not gone very far in assimilating and diffusing the technology of the Industrial Revolution, let alone in contributing to it. Mining, engineering, and textile know-how came predominantly from Britain, chemical know-how predominantly from France and Belgium. Many industries were only on the threshold of mechanization; manufacture in one-man workshops, back yards, and even parlours, under contract to a *Verleger* (factor), was still usual. Many skilled artisans could still prefer the life of a *Wandergeselle* (migrant journeyman) carrying the tools of his trade in a knapsack to that of a factory operative.

These Arcadian conditions did not last much longer. The depression of the 1870s hit most severely the least-capitalized and least efficient producers. From the 1880s onwards, mechanization, size of unit, and productivity commanded the direction and pace of industrial

Table 3.1 Industrial Development, 1850–1913

	Germany	France	UK
		(million metric tons)	
Coal Production			
1850	5.1	4.5	57.0
1871	29.4	13.3	118.0
1890	109.3	26.1	184.5
1913	191.5	40.8	292.0
Pig Iron Production			
1850	0.2	0.4	2.2
1871	1.5	1.4	6.5
1890	4.7	2.0	8.0
1913	14.7	4.6	11.0
Steel Production			
1850	—	—	—
1871	0.2	0.1	0.3
1890	2.2	0.6	3.6
1913	17.9	4.6	7.8

growth. This was particularly true of the two industries to which Germany made the greatest technical contributions, the chemical and the electrical.

A natural advantage—the extraordinarily rich deposit of potassium salts at Stassfurt, between Magdeburg and Halle—and an educational one—the high standard of scientific knowledge—enabled Germany, when the time came, to snatch the chemical lead from Britain and Belgium, who had, in this as in every other field, started first. By the 1880s Badische Anilin at Ludwigshafen, Bayer at Leverkusen, AGFA in Berlin, and Hoechst near Frankfurt were giants by world standards. Their most spectacular success was in dyestuffs. By the turn of the century they provided 90 per cent of world exports.

But it was the electrical industry which saw the greatest of all achievements. Its founder was the technician-entrepreneur Werner von Siemens, who in 1867 invented the dynamo and in the 1870s was experimenting with electric traction. Resting on American as well as German inventiveness, Germany's electrical factories became leading producers of equipment for lighting, heating, generating, and transmitting. They quickly concentrated themselves in two giant combines: Siemens-Schuckert and Emil Rathenau's Allgemeine Elektrizitäts-Gesellschaft (AEG). These two companies were paradigms of the way Germany had developed industrially: a belated start, a rapid rise based on technological excellence and rational organization, well-financed consolidation of production, and an emphasis on quality. As a reward the German electrical industry in 1913 provided a third of the world's output and more exports than Britain and the USA combined.

The years 1873–1914, then, were the years when Germany's industrial base was laid, when she turned from a predominantly rural country into a manufacturer second only to the USA. What happened to Germany in those years—'industrialization'—is what has happened to most European states, and what most non-European states would like to happen to them. The process is easily recognizable and has certain standard features: the movement from country into town, the concentration of production in fewer and larger units, the manufacture for a market instead of for subsistence or local consumption, the tendency for society to divide into those who provide or manage the increasingly large capital needed for sophisticated plant and those who provide labour in return for a wage or a salary. Yet it is equally evident that industrialization does not happen in a vacuum, that it can follow very different courses in Japan or Sweden, in Brazil or the United States. This is partly a function of *when* it happens: clearly a country which takes off in the second half of the twentieth century does so rather differently from one which did so in the first half of the nineteenth. It is also a function of climate, natural resources, and access to trade routes. But it is also very much a function of the existing structure of society, for this will determine how that society absorbs the industrializing process. Hence we must look not only at, but beyond, the form that the Industrial Revolution took in Germany if we want to understand the particular cultural malaise and political frustrations that characterize the Wilhelmine Empire, if we want to explain the dissonance between the economic dynamism of the *Reich* and the relative stagnation of its social norms and political institutions.

There were, indeed, many explanations. There was, in the first place, the speed and thoroughness of the industrialization compared with that of France or the Anglo-Saxon countries. In Britain something like a century elapsed between the first large-scale application of steam power to manufacturing and the climacteric of industrial growth: the process took place in stages, one industry at a time. In Germany it took place in, at most, forty years and in those forty years it covered more ground. There was therefore less chance for mental adjustment to new conditions, for permeating society with ideas of a new type of man.

Secondly, and even more importantly, Britain was already better prepared for the social impact of industrialization at the beginning of that process than was Germany. There were undeniably distinctions of class in eighteenth-century England, but these were not distinctions of caste. The dividing line between landed and commercial wealth was far from clear, and no bar to intermarriage. The ideas that social betterment was admirable, that the pursuit of financial gain was a public service, and that competition for these gains should be maximized were widely known and widely accepted, so that when prosperity grew under free trade and *laissez-faire* the empirical evidence served merely to reinforce the validity of these ideas. Thus the competitive spirit could be transferred from the economy to other spheres of life, bringing about a general tendency towards equalization, not indeed of wealth or social station but of opportunity—in politics through the extension of the franchise, in the public service through replacing connection with examination, in education by dismantling the privileges of the Church of England. Above all, the distinctions between town and country were well on the way to breaking down, principally because by 1800—or at the latest 1840—little remained of the distinctively peasant class characteristic of continental Europe. The farmer, whether landowner, leaseholder, or tenant, was an entrepreneur, improving his capital stock, buying machinery, employing labour like any other businessman. What applied to Britain applied even more strongly to the United States where, outside the slaveholding South, there was no aristocracy. A public ideology based on mercantile values and a civil religion that preached political equality meant that American society was better prepared for the impact of industrialization than any country in Europe.

German industrialization, in contrast, hit a society in which the stratifications of an older epoch were still firmly implanted, and in which the intellectual and literary resistance to the doctrines of Manchester were strong. As we have seen, the first phase of industrialization favoured the process of unification, but the outcome of the wars of unification reinforced the position of the army, the landowners, the monarchy, and the Prussian constitution—all of them forces hostile to the values of industrial society, all of them entrenched in institutions which one would otherwise have expected to give way to bourgeois onslaught. But not only did they not give way, they were confirmed in their primacy by the course of internal politics from 1878 onwards.

The willingness of so many of the makers of the Industrial Revolution to accommodate themselves to the pre-industrial social and political order sprang partly from fear of social unrest. But it sprang also from the effect on the industrialists and the middle classes of the experience of unification—the respect for the state, the worship of force, and the craving for social unity which it enhanced. The individualistic materialism preached by the economists and political scientists of capitalism in Britain, France, and the United States seemed destructive of the social fabric. 'It is not peace and human happiness that we have to bequeath to our descendants', said Max Weber in his inaugural lecture at Heidelberg in 1893, 'but the preser-

vation and cultivation of our national peculiarity . . . the social unification of our nation that modern economic development has blasted
asunder'. And Weber ranked as a modernizer.

Above all, the speed and technical thoroughness of the whole
process left their mark. The German Industrial Revolution was the
work of a very few men, who soon dominated the entire economy.
There was no transitional period during which a large number of small
and medium-sized factory owners was characteristic of manufacturing
industry; they existed, certainly, but their role was subordinate. Very
quickly, the giant firm towered above them. In 1910 there were 50,000
joint-stock companies in Britain, 5,000 in Germany. But the average
capitalization of the German firms was three times that of the British.
Krupp's of Essen employed nearly 70,000 men, the Siemens of Berlin
over 57,000. Not only was the capitalist class small, but far fewer
Germans than Britons had a stake in industry through direct investment. After the speculative mania of the *Gründerzeit* (promoters' era)
most Germans preferred to put their savings into banks and government bonds, and it was from the banks that industry got the credit it
needed for its expansion.

The rather privileged position which these captains of industry
acquired explains why, although they were obviously motivated by a
strong competitive impulse, they did not behave as though they were.
They showed this in their attitudes towards their rivals, their employees, and the state. Towards their employees many of them displayed
the conscientious, autocratic paternalism of the Prussian state. Krupp
provided housing estates and health services for his employees well
before the end of the century; in return they were expected to place
loyalty to the firm first; and many of them did, boasting of their often
hereditary status as 'Kruppianer'. The most extraordinary of the
Wilhelmine tycoons was Baron Carl von Stumm-Halberg, the Saar
coal and steel magnate, Conservative Reichstag member and personal
friend of the Emperor. He forbade his employees to belong to or
recruit for the Social Democratic Party, to belong to any trade union
(even a Christian one), or to subscribe to any non-Conservative news-
paper. They could not marry unless they were at least twenty-four
years old, had personal savings, and had submitted the bride for
approval. Their children had to go to church.

This militant hostility to Socialist and even Liberal 'subversion' was strongest in heavy industry, which had indeed taken the initiative towards tariffs and alliance with the state in the 1870s. The iron, coal, and steel firms now took the lead in fashioning a development which was by no means unique to Germany but which became dominant there as nowhere else: the cartel. The cartel is not a merger of hitherto independent firms, nor is it a 'trust' of the American type, with its interlocking shareholdings. It is simply an association of manufacturers who come to a contractual agreement about the level of production and the scale of prices. As such it can acquire a monopolistic grip on a basic commodity. After the turn of the century the Rheinisch-Westfälisches Kohlensyndikat controlled almost the entire Ruhr coal and coke output and about half that of Germany. The two electrical giants, Siemens and AEG, came to an effective price-fixing agreement. The most famous of all the cartels, I. G. Farben of the chemical industry, did not formally come into being until after the First World War.

The German cartel did not meet with the hostility that industrial concentration evoked in Anglo-Saxon countries and its agreements were upheld as valid by the courts. There were no 'trust-busting' campaigns; 'restraint of trade' was not a term of abuse. Most Englishmen and Americans, but few Germans, would have assumed the self-evident truth of Adam Smith's remark that 'people of the same trade seldom meet together, even for merriment or diversion, but the conversation ends in a conspiracy against the public'. It was not only the comfortable profits that they secured for their participants that made the cartels attractive. They expressed the German ideal of *Gemeinschaft* (community), as opposed to the materialistic, contractual *Gesellschaft* (society) favoured by the Western nations. They represented the final stage of national economic unification, a triumph over the *Kleinstaaterei* (petty provincialism) of the individual firm. They also protected not only the owners but the employees against the extremes of world price and demand fluctuations, and were therefore welcomed not only by the 'professorial socialists' but by some trade union leaders as well.

Yet the welcome which this dynamic but non-competitive capitalism got was symptomatic of the failure of Wilhelmine Germany to develop into a society fully attuned to the new industrial structure, of the strange schizophrenia which affected much of the middle class on the subject of modernity. On the one hand they were proud of Germany's achievements and indeed wanted more of them—objectives to which further industrial growth were essential. On the other hand their social and aesthetic ideals were predominantly pre-industrial and pre-capitalist, a tribute to the tenacity of the older social forces, but also to the failure of the new to capture the imagination. Literary taste, and the place of the city in literature, are good indicators of this. One looks in vain for a German Dickens or Arnold Bennett, a German Balzac or Flaubert. Certainly these novelists were not uncritical towards city life, but they accepted it, sometimes even rejoiced in it. The German literary hero, in contrast, was not (in Oswald Spengler's phrase) the *Asphaltmensch* (creature of the pavement) but the *Schollenmensch* (creature of the soil). The best-sellers of the day were works of rustic sentimentality: Gustav Freytag's *Soll und Haben* (*Debit and Credit*), Wilhelm Raabe's *Der Hungerpastor* (*The Poor Pastor*), Wilhelm von Polenz's *Der Büttnerbauer* (*The Farmer from Büttner*), C. F. Meyer's *Jürg Jenatsch*, or Hermann Löns's *Der Wehrwolf.* What is more sinister, all these works, in contrast with the more lyrical ones of Berthold Auerbach or Annette von Droste-Hülshoff, mixed sentimentality with brutality. Either they extolled nature red in tooth and claw (Löns), or they made the peasant hero a covert or overt nationalist symbol, or they provided the Jew as an object of hate—Veitel Itzig in *Soll und Haben*, Moses Freudenstein in *Der Hungerpastor*, Samuel Harassowitz and Isidor Schönberger, who drive Polenz's hero to suicide.

Equally popular, and of more direct political influence, was a work of non-fiction which first appeared anonymously in 1891: Julius Langbehn's *Rembrandt als Erzieher* (*Rembrandt as Educator*). It was an appeal to youth, against the pomposities of village inn politics, against the emptiness of 'official', academic art, against the fact collecting of German scholarship. 'The professor', he wrote, 'is Germany's national disease'. Much of what he denounced needed denouncing, not least the opulent vulgarity of the *nouveaux riches* of Berlin. He was not alone in speaking up for sensitive youth against their uncomprehending elders and it was a highly necessary advocacy. In

Prussia alone, between 1883 and 1889, 110 schoolboys committed suicide. But his contemporary Frank Wedekind, who wanted to emancipate the individual through frankness about sex and the emotions, and whose importance is now recognized in literary history, broke too many of the taboos of the day; his works were execrated and their performance banned. Langbehn, on the other hand, prescribed old remedies for new complaints. The peasantry: 'The provinces will have to be mobilized, politically as well as spiritually, against the capital . . . the new German art will have to base itself on the peasantry'. Social stratification: 'A social aristocracy resting on traditional historical conditions and therefore at one with the healthy elements of the lower classes . . . the principle of corporative organization which is now gradually returning to favour in Germany'. Ethnic purity: 'The Germans of today . . . ought to be that which they were from long ago . . . they are, were, and will be Aryans'. But he was a prophet, too. Dissatisfied with their present political leaders, Germans yearned for their 'secret emperor', an artist-dictator: 'a Caesarlike, artistic individual, powerful and spiritually overwhelming'.

By 1918 the book had sold 150,000 copies. It addressed the idealism and the frustrations of middle-class youth. It became the bible of the strangest of all the products of industrial Germany, the Youth Movement. This began in 1897 among a group of schoolboys and sympathetic teachers in the Berlin suburb of Steglitz. They, too, wanted to turn their backs on the city, by hiking, climbing, and mountaineering. By 1913 they had thousands of followers, of whom the best known were the *Wandervögel* (birds of passage) troops. They encouraged folk-songs, madrigals, and amateur dramatics. They avoided tobacco, alcohol, elaborate, unhealthy clothing, and all luxuries. And yet, as Charles Péguy pointed out, 'Tout commence en mystique et finit par politique.' In an Anglo-Saxon context these solemn devotees of raw carrots, guitars, and homespun clothes would most likely be pacifist, internationalist, anti-authoritarian, scanning the latest Fabian pamphlet or issue of the (old-style) *New Republic* round the camp fire. In the Wilhelmine context they were almost invariably nationalist and reactionary. To reject the effects of urbanization and industrialization meant—unless one was a working-class Marxist—rejecting the institutions and assumptions of industrial society. The innocuous wanderings to the forests, castles, and half-timbered towns, the revivals of folk dances were a search for a past that could heal the divisions of the present: the static, idealized past of Hans Sachs's Nuremberg or Goethe's Weimar. The more ambitious tours abroad were often visits to scattered German-speaking minorities in the Habsburg monarchy or the Russian Empire. This *völkisch* solidarity applied equally to the movement's own composition; very few groups accepted Jewish members. In sexual matters they took their cue from Langbehn rather than from Wedekind: the flight from the city was a flight from Babylonian erotic stimulation into the imagined purity of asceticism. The youth movement was, at any rate before 1918, an overwhelmingly male phenomenon. And though they despised the politics of state secretaries and Reichstag parties, they did so to show that they were the true patriots. When the various youth organizations joined together for a festival on the Hohe Meißner mountain, the date they chose was the centenary of the defeat of Napoleon at the battle of Leipzig—11 October 1913. And they proclaimed their ideals in impeccably military language:

We want to continue to march in separate formations, but conscious . . . of fighting shoulder to shoulder.

The Emperor and the Regime

The search for spiritual unity, whether in admiration of the past, or in cultural nationalism, or in the disavowal of practical politics, showed how strong were the fissiparous trends in the lands that the Prussian army had unified. What Germany lacked was, in Langbehn's phrase, an 'inner Sedan'—some momentous event which would do for popular loyalties what the defeat of Napoleon III had done for the state. Wise political leadership could have contributed to the slow evolution of an unspoken consensus, yet it is precisely this that the Empire lacked. Bismarck had certainly been a popular hero, but the contempt in which he held public opinion and the brutality with which he treated antagonists did little to lessen the distance between ruler and subject, or to diminish the mixture of fatalism and cynicism with which most citizens regarded authority.

Wilhelm II was equally ill qualified for coaxing his subjects into the habits of mature citizenship, but for different reasons. He was, according to Professor Michael Balfour, 'the copybook condemnation of the hereditary system': his intelligence, his conscientiousness, even his geniality came out when, after his abdication, he lived in Holland for twenty-two years as a country gentleman with archaeological tastes. But when he became Emperor, at the age of twenty-nine, he felt more inclined to give free rein to the qualities he had inherited from his military grandfather and his Calvinist tutor, Georg Hinzpeter, than to those which he owed to his Liberal father and his rather domineering, enlightened mother (Queen Victoria's eldest daughter). His drive for self-assertion, coupled with his evident immaturity, led him to that stream of indiscretions and faulty judgements to which some observers ascribed all the misfortunes of his thirty-year reign. He took a personal, interfering interest in almost every subject from ship design to theatrical productions. His love of military ceremonial verged on the pathological. Count Zedlitsch-Trützschler, a senior court official, noted in 1904, 'At the moment we are witnessing the thirty-seventh alteration of uniforms since the accession to the throne'. Helmuth von Moltke, the Chief of the General Staff, complained of the uselessness of war-games in which the Emperor always won. He poked the ribs of senior officers doing their physical exercises on his annual cruises. He slapped the Tsar of Bulgaria on the posterior at a public reception. He annotated official papers—intended for further circulation—with such marginalia as 'gemeiner Schuft' (common blackguard), 'elender Lügner' (miserable liar), 'Ochs' (ox), 'Esel' (ass), and 'Kamel' (camel). He sent his ministers autographed portraits with messages such as 'Suprema lex regis voluntas' ('The will of the king is the highest law'). He publicly denounced the Social Democrats as 'vaterlandslose Gesellen' ('scoundrels without a fatherland') and the leader of the Zentrum as needing 'einen Tritt in den Arsch' ('a kick in the arse'). He surrounded himself at court with dubious personalities like the expatriate racialist theorist Houston Stewart Chamberlain, who had married Wagner's daughter, and the homosexually inclined spiritualist Phillip von Eulenburg, whose companion, General Cuno von Moltke, referred to the Emperor as 'das Liebchen' ('darling'). In 1907 the journalist Maximilian Harden published a number of scandalous allegations (never conclusively proved) against these two in his periodical *Die Zukunft*, but to little effect; the next year the chief of the military cabinet, Dietrich von Hülsen-Häseler, collapsed and died while performing for the Emperor dressed as a ballerina.

These episodes would have mattered less had they been restricted to Wilhelm's private life. But his refusal, indeed inability, to distinguish between the private and public spheres made him susceptible to intrigue and gossip and led him into disastrous errors of judgement. Yet it is difficult to accept his undoubted eccentricities as the alibi for the political mistakes of the Wilhelmine period, for no man, however powerful, can act alone, and Wilhelm acted within the admittedly ill-defined constitutional framework he had inherited. It was under Wilhelm that the question which his grandfather and Bismarck had always succeeded in smothering was increasingly, and publicly, asked: who governs in Berlin?

The unique, though by no means always smooth, relationship between Emperor and Chancellor that prevailed until 1888 could not outlast these two men. It was not only the obvious incompatibilities of character that estranged the new Emperor and the old Chancellor almost from the beginning. Bismarck had, after all, saved the old Emperor's crown: his grandson owed him no such debt. The other kings and princes of Germany, by contrast, owed nothing to the new Emperor: there was a distinct risk that under him lack of respect for the central authority might have a disintegrative effect.

In addition to all this, Bismarck and Wilhelm II did not see eye to eye on several important policy issues. As Bismarck grew older, he grew more obstinate in his obsessions. This meant, in domestic policy, a growing fear of Social Democratic subversion, so that he began to toy with at any rate the possibility of a *coup d'état* against parliament, should it fail to comply with his wishes. It meant in foreign policy an increasing dependence on the Russian connection, exemplified by the 1887 Reinsurance Treaty, despite growing signs of Russian dissatisfaction with this arrangement. Wilhelm, on the contrary, wanted to drop the repressive legislation against the Labour movement, not because he was a convinced democrat but because he saw himself as a People's Emperor with an understanding of the social question. He also wanted to break the Russian link, which inhibited his expansionist ambitions and his desire for better relations with Britain. Given these incompatibilities, it was evident that anyone with a grievance against Bismarck would be tempted to insinuate himself into the entourage of the Emperor, who was soon surrounded by a very heterogeneous coalition. Some, like the alleged 'grey eminence' of the Foreign Office, Friedrich von Holstein, tried to influence him because they feared Bismarck was losing his grip and staking too much on Russia; some, like the arch-Conservative Chief of the General Staff, Alfred von Waldersee, because they hoped for high political office; others, like Eulenburg, because intrigue flattered their self-importance.

In the event Bismarck engineered his own downfall sooner than his enemies, or the Emperor, might have wished. The compact parliamentary majority of the *Kartell*—Conservatives and National Liberals—which he had used to get through the septennial army estimates in 1887 disintegrated when he insisted on the renewal of the anti-Socialist legislation, which even the parties of the Right now viewed with increasing scepticism. The outcome of the 1890 elections, in which the *Kartell* parties were heavily defeated, left him without a majority unless he were to turn to the Zentrum, whom the new Emperor distrusted. This domestic defeat coincided with the need to renegotiate the Reinsurance Treaty, and this dual crisis culminated in the disastrous final meeting between Wilhelm and Bismarck on 15 March 1890. The Emperor accused the Chancellor of constitutional improprieties, whereupon Bismarck quoted to Wilhelm a letter in which the Tsar called him 'un garçon mal élevé de mauvaise foi' ('a badly brought up boy of bad faith'). It was a bad card to play. It confirmed Wilhelm in the anti-Russian course on which he was determined to embark and which he emphasized in the public letter to his Chancellor that left Bismarck no choice but to resign. Yet, on the day he wrote that letter, a Russian delegation arrived in Berlin to discuss treaty renewal.

Bismarck left office, after twenty-eight years of continuous service, for the same reasons that he had entered upon it. He was determined to save the Prussian monarchy, if necessary against parliament, if necessary against the wishes of the monarch. Habituated to compliance from one whose nominal servant he was, he was incapable of accepting a view of the state's interests that differed from his own. The moment the monarch determined to press such a different view, his position became untenable, for he had—deliberately—refused to create those political institutions—party government, or an Imperial cabinet—that would have given him a base for resisting.

So Bismarck's resignation opened the question: who governs? but did not settle it. The beginnings of an answer were suggested by the brief course of his successor's chancellorship. General Leo von Caprivi was an intelligent, honest, dignified public servant with no previous political experience. He wanted to stand above parties and above interests, unaware that there are no impartial, disinterested solutions to political questions. He discovered very quickly that public life was full of lobbies and factions who were determined, and able, to interpose their veto the moment Government policy went against them. He negotiated trade treaties with Eastern European states, in return for which he had to lower Germany's grain duties. This pleased industrial exporters and urban consumers, but it displeased the agrarian lobby. He attempted to reform local government in eastern Prussia, again at the expense of the landowners. He allowed Polish language instruction again, for the first time since the *Kulturkampf*, in the schools of Polish-populated Prussian areas. He signed a treaty with Britain, exchanging Zanzibar for Heligoland. Equally alarming were the parliamentary majorities on which Caprivi depended for some of his measures. The trade treaties got through only with the votes of the Social Democrats, the 1893 military budget only with the votes of the Poles, 'enemies of the *Reich*' both of them.

It began to look as though everything that the Right had achieved since 1878 was once more in danger. The agrarians, already well organized, launched a counter-attack through the creation, in 1893, of the Agrarian League. Though its leadership was, as in the bodies that preceded it, aristocratic, it managed to recruit large numbers of peasant farmers from the western parts of the *Reich*. And though its immediate task was to drive Caprivi from office and reverse his tariff policy it soon became an important ideological pressure group on behalf of conservatism and nationalism, with a membership of nearly 300,000. It was wealthy, which the political parties were not. It endorsed or denounced parliamentary candidates according to their stand on individual issues. Its members sat not only in legislatures but in ministries. It published national newspapers which spread its ideas beyond the immediate circle of paid-up members. In its agitational, demagogic practices it deliberately modelled itself on the Social Democrats and aimed at being their right-wing counterpart.

By 1892 Caprivi had become so frustrated at the need to cope with the internal politics of Prussia that he resigned the Prussian premiership (though remaining, like Bismarck, Prussian Foreign Minister). The immediate cause had been the Emperor's refusal to support him in resisting a school bill that restored some Church influence in public education. Two years later the Emperor stabbed him in the back on an Imperial matter: an anti-Socialist bill that the new Prussian Prime Minister Botho von Eulenburg had prepared and which Eulenburg had insisted should cover the whole *Reich*. Wilhelm publicly supported the bill, although its terms were unacceptable to Caprivi.

Faced with the enmity of both the Prussian Conservatives and the Emperor, Caprivi could no longer remain in office. Under his successor, Chlodwig von Hohenlohe-Schillingfürst, the Emperor's triumph over the chancellorship was consummated in circumstances more humiliating than any Caprivi had endured. The occasion this time was a bill to establish public hearings at courts martial, which had the unanimous support of Hohenlohe and the Prussian cabinet. The bill would not only remove a widely felt grievance but would make it easier to get supplementary military funds out of the Reichstag. The Emperor, under pressure from the army, was bitterly opposed to the bill and refused to give his consent to it even after Hohenlohe had, in 1897, persuaded the Reichstag to part with the additional money by promising that the bill would be presented. Had Hohenlohe then resigned, the inexorable subordination of his office might have been halted. But he felt that to hang on was the lesser evil. He did, in fact, get the bill—or most of it—in 1899, but by then the damage had been done.

That Bismarck would have no successor was thus clear in the year before his death. But the episode of the Canals Bill demonstrated that even the Emperor's authority could not prevail against the resistance of those who paraded their loyalty most loudly. The admittedly expensive project to extend Germany's canal network by linking the

Rhine and Elbe systems had obvious economic advantages. It had the enthusiastic support of Wilhelm, who loved grandiose public works. It was less welcome to the Junkers. They did not care for the expenditure of public money for the benefit of industrialists; they feared that the canals would lure labour from and raise wages in the eastern provinces; they calculated that the canals would facilitate food imports. Since the project was a purely Prussian one its fate had to be settled in the Prussian Landtag, which the Conservatives dominated. It was defeated when first introduced in 1898, despite the Emperor's support and despite the fact that many of the Conservative deputies were public officials and therefore subject to pressure. They were able to blackmail Wilhelm because, now that he had turned his back on his ministers and on the parties of the Reichstag, he could govern only through them. If he dissolved the Landtag to get his way he ran the risk of a Liberal majority in Prussia; and this reminder of 1862 he wanted even less than they wanted canals.

What this interlude, like the one over the courts martial, demonstrated is that in the twenty-year-old alliance between industry and Old Prussia, Old Prussia was the senior partner. In the country which dominated the production of the world's most advanced electrical and chemical goods, in which Gottlieb Daimler and Carl Friedrich Benz had just manufactured the world's first marketable automobile, the old aristocracy, dominating the land, the army, and the bureaucracy, could achieve notable rearguard victories. It owed the ability to do so to the protective tariff, which not only ensured the income of agriculturists but stabilized their numbers. True, those employed in agriculture dropped from 42 to 34 per cent between 1882 and 1907, but this was still an enormous proportion in the light of the country's industrialization. In Britain the proportion was under 10 per cent.

Neither of Hohenlohe's peacetime successors, Bernhard von Bülow (1900–9) and Theobald von Bethmann Hollweg (1909–17), was inclined to question the Emperor's prerogatives; each, in his different way, tried instead to 'manage' him. Bülow's attempts at management, however successful initially, failed at the first major clash between Emperor and Chancellor. By the time this happened Bülow had already suffered a major defeat in the Reichstag, as we shall see in the next section. What sealed his fate was an incident that epitomized

Wilhelmine political life. On 28 October 1908, the London *Daily Telegraph* published an interview with the Emperor which contained a number of egregious indiscretions on the follies of British foreign policy and his own misunderstood role as a friend of Britain. In the Reichstag Bülow admitted that he had approved of the interview, though without reading it, and agreed that the Emperor's choice of words was unfortunate. But it was the Emperor who reaped the constitutional benefit. Bülow's resignation merely accelerated the downgrading of the chancellorship, and the Reichstag, which had attempted to call the Government to account, went away empty-handed. If there was a challenge to the authority of the Government in the remaining years of peace it came, surprisingly, from the Reichstag, and this was attributable to the rapid rise of the Social Democratic Party. The party had emerged from the period of repression with its organization tightened and its morale fortified by martyrdom. In 1893 it polled a quarter of the popular vote, in 1903 over 30 per cent. In 1912 it became the largest party in the Reichstag, with over one-third of the vote. The changing party structure, along with the growth of pressure groups, was the main reason why ruling the Empire became increasingly difficult in the last years of peace. As a result the Government found it increasingly difficult to patch up working majorities for getting its legislation through.

The Evolving Constitution

'Who governs?' was not the only constitutional question to be solved as the Empire reached maturity. It was as important to ask, 'How is it to be governed?' The letter of the Imperial constitution remained unaltered until 1918, but the conventions of political life changed significantly.

Imperial authority inexorably gained at the expense of that of the states. This happened not only because of Germany's greater role on the world stage, but because domestically the functions of the *Reich* Government expanded, while those of the states remained largely static. We have already seen that one major change was the Imperial Government's growing role as the regulator of social and economic life. The social insurance schemes were Imperial measures; tariffs, whether on industrial or agricultural goods, were Imperial issues; by the turn of the century both the criminal and the civil law had been codified at the Imperial level; above all, the military and naval status of Germany were Imperial questions. The state secretaries who ran the Imperial departments, while still nominally subordinate to the Chancellor as they had been in Bismarck's day, were behaving more and more like independent ministers. The new responsibilities of the central government cost money and the increasing budgetary difficulties of the Empire were one of the symptoms of systemic crisis after the turn of the century.

Added to these functional changes came the political maturing of the population. Urbanization, better communications, the influence of education and military service gradually wore down provincial isolation and helped to bring about the beginnings of a German, as opposed to Prussian or Bavarian, political identity. By the 1890s more thoroughly structured political parties and, as time went on, professionally led interest groups articulated an increasingly vocal public opinion. The pioneers of the new-style mass-membership party were the Social Democrats (SPD), released after 1890 from the constraints of the anti-Socialist law, whose following grew, as we have seen, by leaps and bounds thereafter. To compete with them the non-Socialist parties had to adapt and to abandon their traditional reliance on local notables for leadership and funds. In any case, a new generation of voters was less and less inclined to defer politically to social superiors. This was shown not only by the growth of the SPD, but by the appearance of ephemeral populist movements, like the anti-Semitic peasant party of Otto Böckel in Hesse, which was more demagogic than earlier movements of the Far Right, such as that of the Court Preacher Adolf Stoecker.

German Social Democracy was, by the turn of the century, remarkable in two respects. By virtue of its size, its strict organization, and ideological sophistication it was a model for much of the Labour movement in the rest of Europe. It also exercised a major influence on the Second Socialist International, founded in 1889, to which it provided much the biggest contingent. Even more importantly, its presence began to haunt the domestic politics of the Empire. Its rivals and opponents did not know what to make of it. Though its programme and its rhetoric proclaimed the strictest revolutionary Marxism and its opponents liked to paint it as the party of subversion, the SPD was in many ways ambiguous about violent change. Subterraneously it continued to provide a home to the Lassallean tradition of the German Labour movement, that of securing social reform by democratizing the state. The more the party secured a mass basis—and by 1913 it had a million members and more than twice that number in the Socialist trade unions—the more it became a part, even if an oppositional part, of the existing state structure. All the party's efforts to isolate the urban working class from contamination with bourgeois ideology— newspapers, sports clubs, evening classes, allotments—did indeed create a hermetic sub-culture whose members shared a *Weltanschauung*, but they also made these members more content to live peaceably within that sub-culture. Moreover, the Bismarckian social security system, though it failed in its aim of changing the workers' partisan allegiance, almost certainly succeeded in softening their hostility to existing society.

Of those within the SPD who questioned the sterility of the orthodox programme the most important was Eduard Bernstein, the father of 'revisionism'. The evidence before his eyes suggested that capitalism was not about to collapse through its internal contradictions. He therefore wanted the party to face the fact that the working class could make considerable gains without revolution, especially if it sought allies among the peasants and the middle class, some of whom were more exploited in Wilhelmine Germany than some of the workers. Accepting the existing state not only meant a painful intellectual readjustment which the majority of the party were unwilling to make, it also meant a revised attitude to German national defence—could the SPD under certain circumstances vote for the military budget?—and even to Germany's colonial ambitions—what good did it do German workers if Britain and France grabbed the best colonies?

While the party continued to affirm its unaltered principles, its practice was frequently revisionist. Though opposed to militarism and above all to the Prussian-led army, it did not deny the principle of national defence, and conceded that defeat by Tsarist Russia would be a disaster to be avoided at all costs. The logical conclusion of this ambiguous stance was the SPD's vote for the war credits on 4 August 1914. In some of the southern states universal suffrage had been introduced for the state parliaments, thus—in contrast with Prussia—enabling Socialists to participate in the work of government in proportion to their electoral strength. They made electoral alliances with the Zentrum and Liberals, exactly as Bernstein had prescribed; they were becoming just another political party. In the Reichstag the situation was not comparable. Yet the SPD's growing representation—83 seats in 1903, 110 in 1912, out of 397—was a symptom of the public mood to which the party could not fail to respond.

Even more impressive than the transformation of the party landscape was the growth of economic and ideological interest groups. Here again working-class organizations led the way, producing by 1914 by far the largest trade union movement in Europe. The strongest union federation, with two and a half million members, was the Free Trade Unions, close to the SPD, but there were also smaller Liberal and Christian federations. The expanding profession of commercial clerks was organized in a number of unions, including the *Deutschnationaler Handlungsgehilfen-Verein* (DHV), with a strong nationalist, anti-Semitic, and anti-feminist ideology, which was the largest of the white-collar unions by 1914. Industrialists had led the way in the creation of pressure groups, having formed the *Centralverband Deutscher Industrieller* (CDI) in 1876 to lobby for duties on iron and steel, but this rather conservative body did not suit the more modern, export-oriented manufacturing sectors, who set up a rival, free-trading *Bund der Industriellen* (BdI) in 1896. The Agrarian League of 1893 has already been mentioned. All of these bodies had greater or lesser links with political parties and in some cases almost dominated their party patrons. The Agrarian League was inseparable from the Conservative Party, the CDI's main connection was with the Reichspartei and the right wing of the National Liberals, and the BdI's with the more left-wing Liberals.

Even more numerous than these economically oriented lobbies were the proliferating ideological groups. On the one hand there were those with a religious basis. The *Gustav-Adolf-Verein*, named after the Swedish king of the Thirty Years' War, aimed to give succour to the mainly German-speaking Protestant diaspora of Eastern and South-

Eastern Europe. The *Volksverein für das katholische Deutschland*, which had over half a million members by 1914, was designed to mobilize the Catholic population for confessional solidarity and as a defence against the temptations of an increasingly secular society. It also acted as an electoral agent for the Zentrum. The Central Association of German Citizens of the Jewish Faith (C.V.) had a more overt lobbying objective, to ensure the implementation of their members' civil rights and to combat anti-Semitism.

An even more influential development was the growth of lobbies to promote ideological ends or particular policy aims. The first of these was the Pan-German League of 1893, founded in response to Chancellor Caprivi's abandonment of the colony of Zanzibar to Britain, but soon expanding its programme to embrace a whole range of ultranationalist and expansionist demands. The Pan-Germans were joined by a Naval League to promote the idea of Germany as a major naval power (of which more in the next section) and by smaller bodies dedicated to backing the army or advocating colonial expansion. A German Peace Society, founded in 1899 by the writer Alfred Fried, was, by contrast, not very successful. Despite their often conflicting aims, all these organizations had one thing in common. They were a symptom of escalating political participation, especially on the part of the middle class. Except for the Agrarian League and the trade unions, with their obvious class bases, the new lobbying leagues drew their membership predominantly from the professional middle class and from the age group that had grown up in the first decades of the Empire and now wished to realize its potential as a Great Power. Some of these bodies, like the Naval League, enjoyed official support, since their aims coincided with those of particular Government departments, but that is not the whole explanation of their popularity, nor of the Naval League's success in recruiting a membership well into six figures. Nor should we be deceived by the rhetoric of some of the more right-wing interest groups, such as the Agrarians or the white-collar DHV, directed at preserving a static social order based on 'estates': whatever their proclaimed objectives might be, they represented mobilized bodies of public opinion that inevitably narrowed the Government's freedom of action. They thus weakened the state even while trying to strengthen it.

It is evident that from the 1890s onwards Germany became more difficult to govern, and not only because the founding partnership of Bismarck and Wilhelm I was no longer at the helm. The more hectic partisanship of election campaigns led to a Reichstag in which the Government could count less and less on supporting majorities; the growing lobbying power of the interest groups put the Reichstag parties under increasing extra-parliamentary pressure. In a crisis Bismarck had always been able to secure a favourable election outcome—in 1878 after the attempt on the Emperor's life and in 1887 on the renewal of the military budget. His successors did not find it so easy.

The parties of the *Kartell*, the only ones really 'loyal to the Empire', never again sufficed after 1890. Chancellors had therefore to include either the Zentrum or the Progressives. In general Bülow and Bethmann Hollweg preferred the Zentrum, with its conservative outlook, and except for two years this 'black-blue' bloc predominated. But the Zentrum exacted a high price for its collaboration and was unhappy about the Government's aggressive foreign policy. When, therefore, it went into opposition—as it did over a colonial scandal in 1907—the Progressives had to be brought in. The new parliamentary majority was the outcome of the election that Bülow fought on the colonial budget—the so-called Hottentot elections—but he won this at a price. His electoral coalition excluded the Zentrum, the normal ally of the Conservatives, and included the Left-Liberal Progressives as well as the National Liberals. His intention was twofold: to incorporate the disaffected section of the middle class in his majority and to use that majority to push through a tax reform that would help to pay for the rising arms bill. Even this modest attempt at rationalizing the method of government aroused suspicion. It seemed to his opponents to be a step towards subordinating policy-making to electoral verdicts. Such a development would not only diminish the authority of the Imperial Government, but sideline the legislative role of the Bundesrat and therefore the influence of the states. The Bavarian representatives in Berlin reported back in alarm that 'we now have a parliamentary system and no longer a constitutional system . . . The principle that majorities were to be taken where one found them, according to circumstances, was abandoned the moment Prince Bülow identified himself with a bloc'.

Bülow's strategy came to nothing. His tax reform, which included the introduction of an inheritance tax, was voted down by the Conservatives, the Zentrum and their allies. The failure of reform confirmed what the Canal and Court-Martial Bills had already shown: the veto of the Right over any reform that diminished their privileges. Already weakened by the *Daily Telegraph* episode he resigned and bequeathed the Empire's unresolved fiscal crisis to his successor, Theobald von Bethmann Hollweg. The fiscal crisis was only part of the larger constitutional stalemate that paralysed the Empire in the years before the war. Because of rising Imperial expenditure the tax compromise elaborated by Bismarck in 1878–9 no longer worked. Far from indirect taxes and excise duties feeding the treasuries of the individual states, as originally agreed, the Empire now ran a budget deficit which it had to counter-balance by borrowing. By 1914 the *Reich* debt reached 5 billion marks and the total public debt, including that of the states and municipalities, amounted to 29 billion marks. The only other way of raising revenue was by indirect taxation, since the Bundesrat was determined to veto any Imperial income tax as infringing the states' prerogatives. But the indirect taxes were increasingly unpopular with urban consumers and indeed many manufacturers. Bülow's failure to reform the tax system was the last straw for many of them. 1909 saw the formation of the *Hansa-Bund*, a broad coalition of bankers, manufacturers, and other middle-class groups to break the stranglehold of the protectionist bloc. In 1911 its leaders took the unprecedented step of hinting that it might be legitimate to vote for a Social Democrat at the forthcoming Reichstag election, where he was best placed to defeat the 'black-blue' parties. The outcome of this campaign was a victory for parties of the Left in 1912. Most Germans were patriotic, loyal to the monarchy, proud of their country's achievements, increasingly willing to accept the nationalist and imperialist slogans with which they were bombarded. At the same time—and this is the only plausible interpretation of the voting figures—they were less and less satisfied with their system of government. They resented the injustice of the Prussian franchise, the privileges of the military, the prerogatives of the bureaucracy, the indirect taxes which hit the poor proportionately more than the rich, above all the high price of food exacted by the Agrarians. The impact of this result on policy was small, but the 1913 budget did contain a provision to tax increments in property values—the first time that the Conservative veto on tax reform had been overturned.

None of these developments broke the constitutional stalemate. Only two reforms could have brought about a fundamental change in the system of government: democratizing the Prussian franchise and making the Chancellor responsible to the Reichstag. As long as the federal structure of the Empire operated at the expense of the one democratic feature of the constitution, the Reichstag, and as long as the internal arrangements of its dominant member state remained undemocratic, thoroughgoing reform was out of the question. This was, however, not the only obstacle to constitutional reform. Germany had no tradition of parliamentary sovereignty. The growing popular discontent with aspects of the Imperial regime did not translate into a consensus in favour of a particular reform programme. There was still a widespread acceptance of a separation between executive and legislative authority, as generally understood in nineteenth-century continental constitutionalism. That acceptance was reinforced by an emphasis, as formulated by Hegel, on the separate spheres of the state and civil society. This doctrine attributed to the state a concern with the general interest and to its servants the function of impartially adjudicating conflicting claims. Parties, in contrast, were the expressions of societal concerns and therefore by definition representative of sectional interests only. Moreover, though most of the parties would have liked more influence, they were not necessarily attracted by the responsibilities of power. The Conservatives, reduced to 9 per cent of the vote by 1912, increasingly saw the unreformed Prussian parliament as their main power base. The Zentrum was reluctant to abandon its pivotal bargaining position under the convention of *ad hoc* majorities; all the non-Socialist parties feared, in the light of the rise of the SPD, that parliamentarization would sooner or later lead to Social Democratic domination. As long as parliament remained subordinate to the executive, the parties had no role as recruiters of political leadership and no incentive to behave in a politically responsible way. As long as the Reichstag had only a negative role to perform, a parliamentary career would be held in low esteem and few men of outstanding quality would be attracted to it. There was therefore a disparity between influence and responsibility. But political parties were at least answerable to their electors; interest groups, often closer to power than the parties, were not necessarily answerable to anyone, nor did they have to bear responsibility for the consequences of their advocacy.

The *Daily Telegraph* affair and the 1912 election did result in attempts to strengthen the rights of parliament. The stronger the Social Democrats became the more they could attempt to use the Reichstag as a 'control' on the executive. They automatically gained representation on its committees and after the swing to the Left in 1912 they secured, in collaboration with the Liberal parties, membership of the presidium of the House, and with it a say in business and procedure. Indeed, a Social Democrat, Philipp Scheidemann, was elected Vice-President of the Reichstag, only to resign rather than be presented at court. The same Reichstag also extended its right to ask questions and debate Government policy. It still could not force the Government to reply—it could not, after all, change the constitution unilaterally—but it could become a more vocal organ of critical opinion than before.

The limits of its powers were graphically illustrated by the Zabern incident of 1913. In this small Alsatian town (now known as Saverne) the local commander had arbitrarily arrested twenty-eight civilians and detained them. The Reichstag censured the Chancellor, who defended the military, with only fifty-five Conservative votes in support of the Government. No action followed this gesture—none could—but it demonstrated once more the gap between the sentiments of an urban, literate population and an insensitive, dynastic Government. The episode also showed that critics of the regime sought reform rather than revolution. They wanted the army to be accountable, but they did not want to undermine it. They had no intention of refusing to pass the military budget, which was the one sanction that was open to them.

Although Germany's rulers were able to resist any calls for significant reforms, the trend of public opinion was ominous for the country's rulers. Murmurs of a *coup d'état* were once more heard, but a more effective counter-move was to attack public opinion head on— to provide alternative attractions and other objectives for political enthusiasm, 'to export the social question', in Holstein's cynical phrase.

It would be foolish to attribute Germany's more expansionist policy after the fall of Bismarck solely to an ingenious publicity stunt. It accorded too closely with the personal inclinations of Wilhelm, and with the interests of industrialists and generals, for that to be true. It would have been pursued even if the Social Democrats had been feebler, or the cartoons in *Simplicissimus* less scabrous. But its utility as social cement was lost on no-one. Johannes Miquel, a National Liberal who was Prussian Minister of Finance in the 1890s and who advocated a *Sammlung* (concentration) of industry, landowners, and the monarchy, emphasized, in his proposals for the Government's 1898 election programme, how public opinion might be diverted from vexations like the Courts Martial Bill:

Colonial policy would turn our minds outward, but it does so only to a certain extent. We must therefore bring other foreign policy issues before the Reichstag . . . Our undeniable successes would create a good impression, and in this way partisan antagonisms would be moderated.

Weltpolitik

Bismarck had to the end thought of Germany as a continental European power. He had no objection to overseas colonies and he could see their commercial value, but he was content to leave their creation to private enterprise. He wanted to restrain France, to control Austria, and to be the partner of Russia. He had no desire at all to compete with Britain. Not merely Wilhelm II but many public figures of the next generation dissented from this view. The link with St Petersburg they regarded as an indignity, a restraint on Germany's freedom of movement. Austria was to be the chief ally in the incipient Teutonic–Slav confrontation. For Wilhelm, in addition, there was the personal ambition of a partnership with Britain to rule the waves and to isolate Russia.

The course of events in the 1890s was to show that the new policy had flaws far greater than the contradictions in the Bismarckian edifice. In the first place, it was not Germany but Russia which gained a free hand when the Reinsurance Treaty lapsed. The tentative approaches of the Boulanger period matured into official negotiations. The French navy visited Kronstadt in 1892; the Paris money market was prepared to supply the loans to Russia which Berlin now refused. In 1894 a formal defensive military alliance was signed between the two countries, reinforced in 1899 so as 'to maintain the balance of power'. This meant, in effect, a French promise to come to Russia's aid in the event of either German or Austrian attack, and a Russian promise, in the event of German aggression, to help recover Alsace-Lorraine. The Germans could afford to be fatalistic about the Franco-Russian alliance as long as there was a prospect of British support. Germany could assert herself with Britain against Russia, or with Russia against Britain. That she succeeded in neither was the consequence, even if not the intention, of *Weltpolitik*, the policy of pursuing world-power status. This policy is particularly associated with two ministers whom Wilhelm was able to appoint in 1897 after his defeat of Hohenlohe—Bernhard von Bülow, who became State Secretary for Foreign Affairs, and Admiral Alfred von Tirpitz, who became State Secretary for the Navy.

Bülow proclaimed the new aims in his first speech to the Reichstag: 'We want to put no-one in the shade, but we too demand our place in the sun . . .'. The trouble with this formulation was that more sunshine for Germany inevitably meant less for Britain. Britain, then the world power *par excellence*, owed her position to her colonies and her navy. Neither the Kaiser nor his advisers wanted to overthrow the British Empire. They wanted to be its equals: 'What was considered right for England is right for us too', wrote the historian Hans Delbrück in the *Preußische Jahrbücher*. But it was precisely this that Britain could not permit. Britain's colonies were not mere blobs on the map, nor her battleships expensive toys, to be accumulated because they were fashionable status symbols. They were the substance of her political power and of her trading profits. Germany embarked on her policy of antagonizing Britain at a time when British opinion, both official and public, was predominantly pro-German. France was still her chief colonial rival, Russia the main threat to her eastern empire: the alliance between the two seemed to compound two traditional dangers. As late as 1898 Britain and France were on the verge of war when their respective patrols met at Fashoda in the Sudan, each laying claim to the headwaters of the Nile. In Britain, as in Germany, there was, under the influence of Darwinism, some support for a racial basis to politics. In 1899 Joseph Chamberlain, the British Colonial Secretary, called for 'a new Triple Alliance between the Teutonic race and the two great branches of the Anglo-Saxon race'. He made a specific offer of a defensive alliance to Germany, even offering to bypass Parliament. But Germany feared that such an alliance would tie her to British influence, and Britain was unwilling to make those concessions over colonies which would have satisfied Germany.

Chamberlain's offer came at a time when the atmosphere between Britain and Germany was already becoming clouded. Wilhelm had offended British public opinion in 1896 when he sent a message of congratulation to President Kruger of Transvaal (the 'Kruger Telegram') after the repulse of the British-inspired Jameson Raid. But the true dimensions of the German challenge outlined themselves in a project whose rationale was to oblige Britain to share her spoils—the building of a navy. 'England', in the words of Tirpitz's decisive memorandum of June 1897, 'is the opponent against whom we need most urgently to have a certain measure of naval power as a factor of political power'. The navy, in Tirpitz's eyes, was to be a lever with which Britain would be forced to respect Germany. No project was dearer to Wilhelm's heart: it satisfied his need (in Bismarck's phrase) 'to celebrate his birthday every day'; it convinced him that it made Germany the arbiter of Britain's external relations ('England approaches us not in spite of, but because of my Imperial navy'), it fed his moods of sulky petulance—'I cannot and will not permit John Bull to prescribe the rate of my naval construction programme'.

Yet the wishes of Wilhelm and Tirpitz did not suffice to produce a navy. Unlike the army, it was not an arm inherited from Prussia; in 1871 it hardly existed. No navy could be built without a Reichstag majority. It was to secure this that Tirpitz organized a vast campaign of publicity and persuasion. The Naval League, aimed at the general public, quickly outstripped the Social Democratic Party in members. Its journal, *Die Flotte*, was selling 300,000 copies within two years. Elite opinion was wooed by the *Flottenprofessoren*, distinguished academics who went on lecture tours. Their names included not only the predictable nationalist contingent but theologians like Adolf von Harnack, classicists like Ulrich von Wilamowitz-Möllendorf, medical men, chemists, biologists. Enthusiasm for the navy was the nearest that Wilhelmine Germany got to a loyalist mass movement, that elusive 'inner Sedan' which would give her antique institutions popular foundations and meet the challenge of the Left on its own ground. Once more diplomatic strategy met domestic exigencies.

The idea of a navy was popular for all the reasons that made the army unpopular. The navy would be German, not Prussian. A navy had been one of the aims of the Frankfurt Parliament, the prospect of suitable naval bases one of the reasons why the Liberals were so enthusiastic for the annexation of Schleswig-Holstein in the 1860s. The navy was predominantly middle class and recruited from Northern and Western Germany. A non-privileged, non-reactionary force of this kind would give even the normally anti-militarist Zentrum a chance to show its patriotism. So, partly thanks to the skill of Tirpitz's propaganda, partly thanks to the way battleships seemed to fill an emotional vacuum in the political life of Germany, the Navy Bill was passed. The Reichstag agreed to an expenditure of over 400 million marks (£18 million or 87 million US dollars), to be further increased on four subsequent occasions, for a project whose purpose was at best ill defined and whose efficacy was at the least questionable.

In the decade before the outbreak of the First World War the naval building programme, in which Britain was determined—successfully—to maintain a lead, was the chief cause of deteriorating relations between the two countries. The failure of Chamberlain's negotiations in 1898, and the humiliations of the Boer War (1899–1902), which left Britain friendless, both contributed to Britain's emergence from isolation. The only alternative to the unavailable 'Teutonic' alliance was an association with France and Russia and this came about, slowly and in stages.

The reconciliation with France was easier, if only because France was now willing to renounce claims to Egypt—disputed with Britain since the time of Napoleon—as the price of Britain's support against Germany. In 1904 the Entente Cordiale—not a treaty with contractual obligations, merely the beginning of a desire to collaborate—was signed between the two states. The architect of the Entente was Théophile Delcassé, the French Foreign Minister, in many ways the true heir of Bismarck. Like Bismarck he saw in Russia's friendship the key to the military dominance of Europe, like Bismarck he saw the need to be *à trois* among the five great powers of the continent. He could secure this superiority only by ending the enmity between Britain and Russia, an ambition achieved in 1907 when these two states also signed an entente. The Triple Alliance of Germany, Austria, and Italy, dating from 1882, was thus faced with a Triple Entente whose military and economic potential was at least its equal. The Entente was, however, an informal grouping with highly flexible relationships; what cemented it was the course of German policy in the years to 1914.

The Anglo-French side of the Entente was fortified by Germany's attempts to split it; the Anglo-Franco-Russian side by Germany's support of Austria and her infiltration of Turkey. Twice, in 1905 and 1911, Germany tried to challenge the Anglo-French share-out of Morocco, one of the bases of the Entente. In 1905 Wilhelm, on a state visit to Tangier, declared his hope for an 'open door' Morocco, with equal chances for German trade, in itself a reasonable demand. The purpose of the speech was to demonstrate to France that she could not collude with Britain against Germany; in fact, the eleven-power conference at Algeciras in 1906, which met at Germany's instance, rejected her case. Five years later, when the German cruiser *Panther* dropped anchor off Agadir, again ostensibly to protect German interests, it was Britain who was more offended than France, for France was beginning to assume an essential role in British balance-of-power calculations.

Having failed to frighten Britain with a navy, Germany tried to weaken Britain by attempting a reconciliation with Russia. Here again, the German Government failed and for the same basic reason; it seriously underestimated the suspicion it evoked by the impulsiveness and inconsistency of its actions. The project for a railway from Berlin to Baghdad—never completed—aroused Russia's fears; so did Germany's noisy support for Austria's annexation of Bosnia and Herzegovina, Turkish provinces in the Balkans that she had occupied militarily in 1878; so did the sending of a German officer to supervise the training of the Turkish army.

Yet if Germany's often incomprehensible initiatives helped to escalate nationalism, aggressiveness, and even hysteria among her antagonists, she was entitled in her turn to complain about some of these reactions. What, after all, was wrong with a place in the sun? Was imperialism a free-for-all, or was it not? Why did Britain view with such envy (Wilhelm's word) Germany's efforts to establish a new balance of power on a world-wide scale? Why the double standard which condemned Germany to her existing sphere of influence while apparently condoning Russia's drive on Constantinople, or French *revanche*, which revived after the second Moroccan crisis with the Lorrainer Raymond Poincaré becoming first Premier, then President?

It was this indignation that constituted Germany's genuine grievance about 'encirclement', and despair about this situation led her policy-makers to think more readily of war as the sole solution. 'If we once more creep out of this affair with our tail between our legs,' wrote Helmuth von Moltke, the Chief of Staff, at the time of Agadir, 'if we cannot brace ourselves to pursue an energetic claim that we are ready to enforce with the sword, then I despair of the future of the German Empire'. Such outbursts do not prove that Germany plotted war, but they do suggest that her leaders were resigned to its inevitability—a fatalism that affected even such non-bellicose men as the Chancellor, Bethmann Hollweg. The political fatalism was compounded by tactical inflexibility. Faced with the risk of a war on two fronts, once the Franco-Russian alliance was a reality, Moltke's predecessor, Alfred von Schlieffen, had perfected a war plan which recognized only this one contingency. Since France was easier to knock out than Russia, the first blow must be struck westwards; since France was more vulnerable from the flank, Belgian neutrality must be violated. Once Paris was in German hands, Russia could be mopped up—provided she wished to fight on alone. The fatal element of this plan was that it deprived the Government of all freedom of manœuvre in a crisis. It was 'militarist' in the crudest sense, in subordinating foreign policy to strategy. It ran completely counter to the *aperçu* of the Prussian army's mentor, Carl von Clausewitz, that war should be seen only as an *instrument* of policy.

These political and military presuppositions were put to the test in the summer of 1914. The assassination of the Austrian heir-apparent, Archduke Franz Ferdinand, at Sarajevo in Bosnia on 28 June was a blow aimed at Austria, not Germany. But Austria's determination to hold Serbia, from where the assassin had crossed the frontier, responsible required the support of her German ally. It was the need to maintain the ally's morale that explained, to a great extent, why the Emperor, the General Staff, and, after some hesitation, the Foreign Office decided to give Austria the famous 'blank cheque' of 5 July: the assurance of Germany's 'full support in an ally's customary loyalty'. Those who issued the cheque knew that Russia might feel obliged to come to the aid of her protégé Serbia, if only to maintain her credit with the Slav nationalists of the Balkans, and that a war with Russia would certainly involve France and possibly Britain. But equally they hoped that Russia would stay out, thus localizing the conflict.

Austria, however, decided to draw fully on the generous account Berlin had opened. She sent an ultimatum in humiliating terms to Serbia and rejected a conciliatory reply. She declared war on 28 July, whereupon Russia made her mobilization—already secretly in train for some days—public. It was a partial mobilization only, directed, like the gunshots of Sarajevo, at Austria, not Germany. But the German Government refused to recognize the distinction, leading the Tsar to order total mobilization on 31 July. On 1 August Germany responded by declaring war against Russia, and on 2 August against France; a German attack on France, via Belgium, put an end to Britain's hesitations. The Entente had become an alliance.

Of all the scholarly debates which have raged in this century among historians, that concerning Germany's 'war guilt' in 1914 has been, and is, the most emotion-laden. Some Germans—soldiers, diplomats, above all the propagandists of the Pan-German League— wanted a war—to gain colonies, to unify the nation, to complete Germany's transition from a continental to a world power. Others, including those in the most responsible positions, failed to do what they might have done to prevent one, because they were convinced that Germany's cause was just, or that war was inevitable, or that if it threatened it was for Germany to wage it at a time, and on terms, most favourable to herself. No-one showed more clearly the constrictions of this self-spun web than the Hamlet-like Chancellor, when he wired to his ambassador in Vienna on 29 July: 'It is solely a question of finding a means of making the realization of Austria-Hungary's aims possible . . . without at the same time unleashing a world war, and if this is in the end not to be avoided, to bring about the best possible conditions under which we may wage it.'

4 War and Revolution, 1914-1919

Our soldierliness has an intimate spiritual connection with our
moralism; indeed, while other cultures have the tendency to
assume civilian forms of cultural behaviour into the most refined
aspects of life, into art, German militarism is in truth the form
and revelation of German morality.

(Thomas Mann, *Thoughts in Wartime*, 1914)

AVERAGE EATER. Well, how are things? How are you coping with
the war?

BIG EATER. I beg you, don't ask. I'd rather you gave me some of
your bread coupons. I collect them wherever I can.

AVERAGE EATER. What an idea, I can't even cope myself. And me
just an average eater! . . . If things go on like this, you can keep
the whole war.

(Karl Kraus, *The Last Days of Mankind*, 1915–17)

Unity under Siege

'I know no parties any longer. I know only Germans', the Emperor
proclaimed from the balcony of his palace on 4 August to the cheering
multitude. Enthusiasm for the war was not restricted to Germany; it
gripped the cities of every belligerent state, as if the war provided a
release from peacetime tensions that were becoming unbearable, as if
hostilities of class, religion, and ideology could now be safely redi-
rected against a unanimously hated foreigner. The impasse which
German political development had reached in the years before 1914
made this release especially welcome, and it seemed to be as welcome
to the opposition as to those who most feared subversion. The key to
this apparent paradox is the dominant role of foreign policy in German
public life, the so-called *Primat der Außenpolitik*.

Of course all states are concerned primarily to preserve their sovereignty and their security; but not all states are so placed that foreign relations are permanently at the centre of public debate. German statecraft has been especially indebted to the legacy of Leopold von Ranke (1795–1886), the father of scientific history, for whom history was the story of struggles between the powers, and for whom 'the supreme law of the state' was self-assertion: 'it imposes the necessity of ordering all internal relationships for the purpose of asserting itself.' This doctrine is welcome to conservatives everywhere, not just in Germany. It emphasizes authority, order, and discipline, habits that conservatives value highly; it enables them to deny civil liberties or social reforms with the claim that these endanger the security of the state. For the same reason the doctrine is unwelcome to the Left. Imperialism, colonialism, militarism, 'power politics' appear as not merely undesirable in themselves, but as instruments of internal repression, covers for authoritarianism. This explains much of the 'little Englandism' of British radicals, or the isolationism of Midwestern Americans.

What made the debate on the sanctity of the state so lopsided in Germany was not so much the existence of a Right, wedded to the primacy of foreign policy, as the absence of a Left, willing to dispute it. Bismarck was able to co-opt the Liberals not least because they, too, wanted a *Machtstaat*—Germany as a great power. The Social Democrats, like the mid-century Liberals, affirmed the principle of national defence; they merely took exception to the Prussian-German army as its instrument. Like the Liberals half a century earlier, they were offered no choice in the matter. In trying to assert the primacy of domestic politics, Liberals and Socialists were therefore fighting with one hand tied behind their backs. This explains the ease with which all parties and all sections of opinion—initially with only negligible exceptions—came together in a national truce, the *Burgfrieden*.

It was not merely the Government, the Conservatives, the Pan-Germans, and those close to them who saw political advantage in the war. The alienated Romantics of the Youth Movement saw in it Germany's spiritual regeneration and their members were among the most enthusiastic volunteers. 'The war has proved the *Wandervogel* right,' wrote Hans Breuer, the compiler of their song-book, in a special preface; 'it has placed its fundamental national idea, stripped of all superfluities, in our midst in all its strength and light. We must become more and more German. . . . Become men, to stand firm and assert your place on the earth.' Many Liberals hoped that the war would at last make Germany into a true nation-state, in which middle-class values would gain equal status. The historian Friedrich Meinecke wrote,

Industrial Germany, with all the masses that it encompasses, has shown its will and its might . . . But the conservative agrarian state, in which the peculiarity of the Prussian state found its social support, has also new, great, and indispensable achievements to its credit . . .

At the same time the unfortunate tensions that existed between the conservative forces of Prussia and the liberal needs of wider Germany have diminished . . .

If our army succeeds in bringing about the full synthesis of people's army and professional army, then in the life of our state the full synthesis of Prussian organism and *Reich* organism can also come about.

The revisionist Socialists equally saw their moderate, evolutionary programme justified: only by co-operating with the Government could they hope to gain recompense for the services of the working class in industry and the army. A week after the war credits had been voted Eduard David, the SPD member who had helped to draft his party's Reichstag statement, recorded in his diary that the war would evoke a democratic as well as a nationalistic wave.

One reason for this consensus was the almost universal belief that Germany was fighting a defensive war. The 'declaration of the 93', signed by Germany's leading intellectuals and ultimately claiming 4,000 subscribers, constituted an appeal to German and world opinion to exculpate Germany from aggressive intent. The belief was particularly important in maintaining the SPD's loyalty to the war effort, which was based on the assumption that the war was not an expansionist one. The case would have been more convincing had not many of the signatories of the declaration given their pens to the crudest hate-propaganda, combining xenophobia and self-satisfaction, in which the war appeared a crusade waged on behalf of superior German culture. Dissenters from this chorus were, initially, few. Albert Einstein was one. Hermann Hesse was another, but his pamphlet *O Friends, not these Tones*, published in Switzerland, with its allusion to Schiller's *Ode to Joy*, did not reflect the temper of the time.

The war was clearly an event that had a profound effect on German national consciousness. What Meinecke called 'the spirit of 1914' was to complete the process begun with the creation of the Empire in 1871. It was to be that 'inner Sedan' that had so frustratingly eluded Germany's publicists and politicians during the long peace. Above all, it gave them an opportunity to emphasize the gap between the soldierly value-system of Prussia-Germany and the mercantile, individualist pacifism of the Western democracies. Thomas Mann, quoted at the head of this chapter, was one of many who proclaimed this message. A more popular version of it came in Werner Sombart's *Händler und Helden* (*Traders and Heroes*):

Only as an Anglo–German war does the war of 1914 gain deeper world-historical significance. The important question . . . to be decided is not who will dominate the seas; much more important is . . . the question: which spirit will prevail, the mercantile or the heroic?

Militarism is the heroic spirit intensified to warlike spirit. It is the perfect union of Potsdam and Weimar . . ., for the 'Eroica' Symphony and the Egmont Overture are surely the most genuine militarism.

The consensus might well have survived had the German armies gained the quick, decisive victory which her military commanders expected. But the German breakthrough in Belgium and Northern France was halted along the Marne in the second week of September, and though Paris came within the range of the heavy guns, this was the nearest the German army ever got to the French capital. From then on the opposing front lines in the West moved for little more than a few miles until the summer of 1918. Repeated attempts by both sides to break through—by the British on the Somme and at Ypres, by the French in Champagne, by the Germans at Verdun and in Artois—came to nothing. In three full years of war (1915 to 1917) the three armies suffered eight million casualties, three million of them Germans.

In contrast, Germany's campaign against Russia went brilliantly, thus doubly falsifying Schlieffen's assumptions. At the end of August

1914 the Germans routed the Russians at Tannenberg, just inside East Prussia; by the end of 1915 German armies had occupied most of Poland. As more powers entered the war, the tide turned even more strongly in Germany's favour. Turkey came in as an ally of the Central Powers, to be followed by Bulgaria; aided by Bulgaria, Austro-German armies occupied most of Serbia in 1915 and most of Romania in 1916. Thus halfway through the war Germany had military control of an area stretching from the Baltic to the Persian Gulf and, more importantly, possession of major wheat and oil resources. Italy, on the other hand, having evaded her obligations to the Triple Alliance at the outbreak of war, joined the Entente Powers in 1915 in return for lavish promises of territorial gains. Though her declaration of war further stretched Austria's tenuous resources, she did badly, suffering the disaster of Caporetto in 1917.

All these successes sufficed to keep Germany going, but not to secure the final victory which both the Government and the General Staff assumed was the one aim worth pursuing. The military impasse had its effects on domestic politics, but these were in an increasingly authoritarian direction. The democratization, which not only Liberals and Socialists but some right-wingers, such as Tirpitz, expected as a natural outgrowth of a 'people's war' did not come. In economic matters the centralized direction worked effectively. Walther Rathenau, son of the founder of the AEG, became the virtual economic dictator of Germany, at the head of the *Kriegsrohstoffabteilung* (Department of Military Raw Materials). Under General Wilhelm Groener and the banker Karl Helfferich, and with the unions' co-operation, complete conscription of labour was introduced. These steps culminated at the end of the war in the agreement between the industrialist Hugo Stinnes and the trade union leader Carl Legien in which the 'social partners' recognized each other's legitimacy and agreed to pool their resources for smooth demobilization. These measures involved a degree of planning, and of associating the major interests with the state, which became familiar enough after the Second World War, but which was not equalled by any of the other belligerents. In part, there were ideological reasons for this: Rathenau's *dirigisme* appealed to the social ideal of *Gemeinschaft* and remained an object of nostalgia long after it had been dismantled.

The parallel growth in political authoritarianism, however, was less popular. In Britain and France the unprecedented degree of government control that the war required was personified by popular civilian politicians, David Lloyd George and Georges Clemenceau, who exercised fairly effective control over the military. Strategy was subordinated to war aims, and both strategy and war aims were open to discussion in parliaments which could, if they wanted to, bring governments down. In Germany, on the other hand, the balance of political power tipped in the opposite direction. The anomalous constitutional provision that the Emperor had sole responsibility in military matters ensured the complete emancipation of the army from civilian control. A state of emergency was declared for the whole Empire at the beginning of the war, but was enforced only spasmodically. The power of the Chancellor was reduced to a shadow when, in 1916, the victors of Tannenberg, Paul von Hindenburg and Erich Ludendorff, were appointed Chief of the General Staff and Quartermaster-General respectively. Of these two Ludendorff, obstinate and conspiratorial, obsessed with reactionary and racialist doctrines, soon became the real dictator of the country. He involved himself not only in the formulation of war aims and overall strategy, but also in domestic and constitutional questions.

Ludendorff was committed to a victory in which Germany would be able to dictate the terms of peace—a *Siegfrieden*. In this he was supported by the Emperor, the army, by many politicians and intellectuals, as well as those who had direct material interests in German expansion—industrialists who coveted the resources of Belgium and France, landowners who coveted the wheatlands of the East, merchants who longed to see British competition removed from Africa and the open seas. Many of the war aims which the German Government now officially accepted coincided closely with the schemes that Pan-Germans and other influential pressure groups had dreamed up before the war; this has led recent historians, notably Fritz Fischer in *Griff nach der Weltmacht* (*Germany's Aims in the First World War*), to conclude that Germany went to war in 1914 with a programme of expansion specifically in mind. That must remain hypothetical. What is demonstrable is that the adoption of an ambitious programme of annexations made Germany deaf to any suggestions of a compromise peace—whether these came from President Wilson, the Pope, or private intermediaries.

One way of securing victory was to break the British naval blockade, which was effectively cutting Germany off from overseas supplies. The one major engagement which the German navy fought with the British—the Battle of Jutland in 1916—failed in this objective. Though more British ships than German were sunk, the British could afford these losses more easily, and the German fleet stayed in port for the rest of the war. The only alternative to an open sea battle was unrestricted submarine warfare, a weapon guaranteed, according to Tirpitz, 'to force England to her knees'. Since this strategy involved sinking any ship making for a British port, including neutral (mainly American) merchant vessels, Bethmann Hollweg resisted it on political grounds. By the spring of 1917, however, Ludendorff, who favoured it, prevailed, and the submarine campaign was launched. Since it coincided with a clumsy German intrigue in Mexico, which was uncovered by the British Secret Service and revealed to the American Government, its principal effect was to bring the United States into the war on the side of Britain and France. But since it also failed to force Britain to her knees, it brought about the most serious political crisis yet in Germany.

Disunity under Siege

The *Burgfrieden* had rested on the assumption that the war was defensive and would end quickly. When neither of these assumptions was borne out, the old political divisions, between those who trusted the German state and those who did not, re-emerged. At first discontent was restricted to the Social Democrats; an anti-war group, dissenting from the majority line, formed itself into an independent party (the USPD) in 1917. Though its core was the old Left, it united, in its leadership, the chief apostles of revisionism (Eduard Bernstein) and orthodoxy (Karl Kautsky), as well as of revolution. By the summer of 1917 discontent had spread across a much wider spectrum of opinion.

On 19 July 1917 the two Socialist parties, the Progressives and the Zentrum, supported a motion that 'the Reichstag strives for a peace of mutual understanding and lasting reconciliation among the peoples'.

This was the coalition of the old Bismarckian *Reichsfeinde*, only this time, thanks to the leftward swing of the 1912 elections, they commanded a majority in the Reichstag. For the first time now they were prepared to use this majority to achieve a policy objective. They created a joint caucus—the *interfraktioneller Ausschuß*—with the short-term aim of bringing about a change of government and the long-term one of imposing parliamentary control on the Chancellor. In their short-term objective they were anticipated by the High Command in a way that illustrated where the power in Germany really lay. Bethmann Hollweg had done his best to keep the Social Democrats within the *Burgfrieden*, fearing social and political chaos if he failed to do so. This meant maintaining public ambiguity about war aims and moving cautiously towards domestic reforms. It was this inclination to 'appease' the Left, as well as his lukewarmness towards the U-boat campaign, that made him unacceptable to the military leaders. The last straw for them was a promise to democratize the Prussian electoral system, which Bethmann had wrung out of the Emperor. Hindenburg and Ludendorff declared that they could no longer retain their commands if Bethmann remained in office. The blackmail worked and a new Chancellor—an obscure civil servant, Dr Georg Michaelis—was in office by the time the Peace Resolution was debated. Parliamentary government seemed further away than ever.

The dragging on of the war broke not only the political consensus but also the social pact. Deteriorating food and fuel supplies were the main reason for the unrest, which first became serious in the spring of 1917, but the revolutions in Russia were also influential. In March 1917 Tsarism was overthrown and a Liberal government took its place. But the Liberals were unable to reverse the military situation and delayed the eagerly expected land reform, so that they in turn were overthrown, in early November, by the Bolsheviks—the left wing of the Russian Social Democratic Party—under Lenin. Fear of Tsarist tyranny had been a major factor in keeping the German workers loyal to the war effort; the removal of this threat made the continuation of the war seem all the more pointless.

But events in Russia also set an example in revolutionary technique. Lenin had seized power by gaining control of the workers' and soldiers' councils—the *soviets*—committees which had sprung up spontaneously to press the claims of the discontented. These councils made their appearance in Germany in January 1918, when, in the depth of the second 'turnip winter', strikes broke out which, in a few days, affected more than a million men. The councils arose out of dissatisfaction with the official, loyalist union leadership; they were led by unofficial shop stewards (*revolutionäre Obleute*) who were to make their appearance again after the military collapse. Significantly, the strikers' demands were political as well as economic: they included democratic government and peace negotiations.

Three and a half years into the war, it was evident that neither the military nor the domestic political objectives of those who were conducting it were within reach. One by one those politicians who were prepared to countenance a peace by negotiation or domestic reform were pushed aside by the military hard-liners. In Germany alone, of the principal belligerents, did the war serve a domestic political agenda. Against those who hoped that the war would democratize the Empire stood the increasingly influential Pan-Germans and the Ludendorff circle, who realized that any move towards democracy would spell death to their military and diplomatic plans and to a peace on their terms.

The result of this development was that the pre-war fault-lines that the spirit of 1914 was supposed to bridge re-opened and deepened. The Left was re-radicalized and sections of the middle class once more alienated by the growing militarization of public life. The Reichstag Peace Resolution and the winter strikes were evidence enough of that. To counter the influence of the Reichstag majority the military and their sympathizers launched a new political party in September 1917, the Fatherland Party, with Grand Admiral Tirpitz as its figurehead. It soon claimed over a million members, more than the SPD. This was the first time that the anti-parliamentary Right was able to mobilize a mass following. The war, it was evident, was polarizing, even revolutionizing German politics. The split on the Left and the emergence of a mass-based Radical Right prefigured the fragmentation and extremism of the party structure in the Weimar Republic. It was neither the defeat, nor the revolutionary uprisings of 1918–19, that wrought this transformation, but the war itself.

Meanwhile the Russian Revolution, though it spurred on the opposition, also gave the Government a respite. Lenin was determined to take Russia out of the war he had opposed all along, and in March 1918 Germany and Russia signed the Peace of Brest-Litovsk. This was a *Siegfrieden* with a vengeance: Russia lost control of Poland, the Baltic provinces, and the Ukraine. It would solve Germany's supply problems and release troops for the West, for a final offensive before the American buildup was under way. Accordingly, Ludendorff launched his greatest attack yet on 21 March. The Entente armies suffered heavy losses and the Germans advanced up to forty miles, their greatest success since August 1914.

It was a Pyrrhic victory. The Allied line re-formed. By July there were a million Americans in France. The Ukrainian crops could not harvest themselves: it took almost as many troops to occupy Russia as it had done to conquer her. On 8 August the Allied counterstroke came. What some of his subordinates had for some time guessed dawned at last on Ludendorff—that the game was up. August 8, he acknowledged, was 'the blackest day of the German army in the history of this war'. He was determined now to make any political concessions necessary to save the German army from total destruction and to maintain, as far as possible, the territorial integrity of the *Reich*.

At a Crown Council on 29 September the generals explained to an astonished Emperor that a cease-fire could no longer be delayed: Bulgaria had already left the war, and Turkey and Austria could hardly last much longer. The time had come, in the words of the Imperial decree of the following day, to share the rights and duties of government with 'men borne on the confidence of the people'. The new people's Chancellor was Prince Max of Baden: his deputy and the state secretaries were drawn from the three parties of the Reichstag majority. It was a revolutionary change, but not a revolution. Parliamentary government came, as national unification and universal franchise had done, as a gift from above.

The task of the Baden Government was to seek an acceptable cease-fire. The best hope for this lay in a direct appeal to President Wilson of the United States, whose programme, contained in the Fourteen Points of January 1918, was one of 'open covenants of peace, openly arrived at', to afford 'political independence and territorial integrity to great and small states alike'. The United States was not formally an ally of the Entente belligerents; she was not bound to recognize the generous promises of post-war gains that the Allied powers had made to each other, and there was no contractual bar to America's seeking a separate peace. But if America was not an ally of Britain and France by treaty, she was one in fact. Wilson insisted that all armistice negotiations must involve all belligerents, that the armistice must not be a cover for a German counter-offensive, that he would be prepared to negotiate with representatives of the people, but not with autocrats and militarists.

Thus the next stage of German democratization was commanded not from Potsdam but from Washington. The constitution of the *Reich* was amended to abolish the executive functions of the Bundesrat, to make the Chancellor and his ministers subject to the confidence of the Reichstag, and to make the Reichstag alone competent in matters of war and peace. By 28 October the German Empire had become a parliamentary monarchy, whose monarch was a ceremonial figurehead. Ludendorff, recognizing a sinking ship when he saw one, asked to be relieved of his command.

Yet, as in September, the Reichstag parties were one step behind events. For the revolution from above, declaring that the old order was untenable, was a signal to the revolution from below. The overwhelming desire of the German populace was now for an end to the war; constitutional amendment was seen as a means, not an end. When, therefore, the order went out on 29 October for the German fleet to set sail, in order to retrieve its honour in a final battle, the crews refused to obey. By 4 November the mutineers were in command of every ship, they controlled the naval base at Kiel, they elected a 'council' and joined forces with the workers' council of the dockyard employees. The revolution spread to every major city. Workers' and soldiers' councils arose spontaneously, the revolutionary shop stewards reappeared. Though the SPD and the USPD tried to gain control of the movement, they had not initiated it. To the left of them the Spartakus-Bund of Rosa Luxemburg and Karl Liebknecht had a revolutionary timetable of its own; but it, too, was overtaken. In Berlin, on 9 November, as a giant demonstration made for the royal palace, Philipp Scheidemann of the SPD proclaimed the German Republic. The

Emperor had already abdicated that morning and left for Holland; Scheidemann acted in order to forestall Liebknecht, who was waiting to proclaim a Socialist republic.

There was now a complete vacuum of political legitimacy. With the Emperor's abdication Max von Baden regarded his mandate as completed, and handed his office to the Social Democrat, Friedrich Ebert. Ebert now formed a government of three SPD and three USPD members. The Berlin workers' and soldiers' council, meeting the next day, expressed its confidence in the new Government, who now gained the title of *Volksbeauftragten* (People's Commissars). It was a government of Socialists, but not a Socialist government. The Spartacists and the shop stewards were not represented in it. The armistice of 11 November met its most pressing need; the questions of public order, of disarming millions of soldiers who had taken the law into their own hands, of reassuring the Allies that Bolshevism was not about to reign in Germany, remained. It was Wilhelm Groener, Ludendorff's successor, who suggested a solution. On 10 November he rang Ebert, confirmed that 'the army places itself at the disposal of his government', and demanded, in return, the maintenance of discipline (i.e. the continued rights of officers) and the combating of Bolshevism. Ebert accepted. The arrangement, secret though it was, was not totally surprising. Groener—a South German, not a Junker—had already gained experience in negotiating with representatives of the Labour movement during the war and the two partners had by now gained considerable respect for each other. And so, with the war at an end, Germany had a cabinet responsible to a Reichstag elected in 1912; a congress of councils which claimed a monopoly of political sovereignty and whose executive (*Vollzugsrat*) set itself up as the watchdog of the cabinet; and a defeated but coherent army whose officers were in secret league with the chairman of the People's Commissars.

The Revolution

Until the spring of 1919 the provisional Government rode out the revolutionary situation, basing itself uneasily on both the enthusiasm of the councils and the coercive power of the still-intact army. Of the

rival contenders for the succession to the Empire the Social Democrats, who headed the Government, had the clearest notion of the
political future they wanted. They wanted a democratic, parliamentary republic. Further details, such as the distribution of property,
could be decided only by a properly elected constituent assembly, not
by a caretaker administration of dubious legitimacy. They distrusted
the councils, whom they regarded as at best agents of chaos, at worst
a stepping stone to Bolshevism. They were not prepared to give up the
semi-autocratic discipline they had evolved in the years of opposition,
and the prestige of the party's name enabled them to retain the loyalty
of the mass of the working class, many of whom might well have
preferred a more radical policy.

The SPD's coalition partners, the USPD, though not, in the
main, opposed to parliamentary government, wanted to retain the
councils as channels of Socialist enthusiasm and instruments of economic democracy. They regarded the tide of public opinion as a
sufficient mandate for the abolition of capitalism. To the left of them,
the Spartacists, who in December renamed themselves the German
Communist Party (KPD), wanted the violent overthrow of the existing order, though without the dictatorship that Lenin had in the
meantime imposed on Russia.

On the political Right the confusion was even worse. The Liberal and Conservative formations simply broke up in demoralization;
only the Zentrum, with its secure confessional roots, survived. The
army, the administration, the judiciary, men almost exclusively with a
stake in the monarchical order, were prepared to support Ebert as
the securest defence against Communism. They were delighted to let
the civilian politicians suffer the odium of the military collapse, of the
armistice, of the disorder and of the prospective peace terms. It was
not long before Erzberger and Ebert were to become the 'November
criminals' who had stabbed the nation in the back.

During December and January there was a race between the
advocates of a national government by councils and those who wanted
the election of a constituent assembly. The national congress of councils was the first to meet. Its composition suggested the continued
readiness of most workers to follow moderate leaders. The SPD were
in a majority and neither Liebknecht nor Luxemburg secured election.

The council congress was thus reduced to being an appendage of the Government, and this accentuated the split in the revolutionary forces: the minority saw itself without a constitutional voice, while the old Imperial officials—civil and military—took their orders from Ebert only, who could thereby sidestep some of the more radical demands. Two incidents, in particular, served to radicalize the Left and, as it turned out, to seal its fate. In mid-December a mutinous naval division held the Social Democratic city commandant of Berlin hostage. Ebert, taking advantage of the hotline to Groener, ordered the army to disarm the mutineers, which its officers were only too anxious to do. To the Left the ensuing bloodshed demonstrated the reactionary character of the Government, and the three USPD ministers, under pressure from their own party, resigned. This clarified the dividing line between pro- and anti-Government Socialists, which the council congress had succeeded in blurring. On the one hand Ebert had a freer hand in the Government, on the other he had to reckon with growing opposition in the streets.

The bitterness of this confrontation was shown in the middle of January when the Government dismissed the extreme Left police chief of Berlin. For a time it looked as though the 'second revolution', the one that would replace bourgeois democracy with the rule of the proletariat, had broken out: by 6 January the centre of Berlin was largely in the hands of revolutionary workers. But the demonstration turned out to be one of spontaneous militancy, led by the shop stewards, without a clear political aim. The leaders of the USPD and the new Communist Party both thought the rising ill timed, though the latter joined in out of loyalty. Ebert dealt with the rising as was now his wont. The regular officers finished it off in a few days, capturing the leaders. On 15 January Liebknecht and Luxemburg were murdered in captivity.

With this event the possibility of subversion from the Left was, for the time being, quashed, the more so as elections to the constituent assembly four days later made the Social Democrats the largest party (SPD 39 per cent, USPD 8 per cent), but did not give the Left the absolute majority which they had rather unquestioningly assumed would be theirs. It opened, however, the possibility of subversion from the Right, and this came from those forces of law and order on which Ebert found himself obliged to rely.

Though Groener and his subordinates continued to offer conditional loyalty to the provisional Government, they were soon without men to command. As the defeated troops reached home they either formed themselves into revolutionary committees or simply disappeared. The officers were therefore obliged to recruit independently, and their natural sources were former regulars, middle-class students, and anyone else with a taste for fighting and a grudge against the Revolution. It was these units, collectively known as *Freikorps*, who were responsible for the deaths of Liebknecht and Luxemburg, who fought Polish insurgents in Silesia and the Bolsheviks in the Baltic states, and who increasingly took it upon themselves to put down political strikes.

The *Freikorps*' major opportunity came in Bavaria. Here, among a presumably inhospitable, largely rural, and Catholic population, Kurt Eisner of the USPD had proclaimed a republic as early as 7 November, and secured the support of both wings of the Social Democratic Party. When he was assassinated by an aristocrat in February 1919, the Munich workers' and soldiers' council established a Soviet-style republic in which power soon passed to the Communist Party. A Communist government in Munich was a threat that Berlin could not tolerate; the Army—which meant the *Freikorps*—was sent to 'restore order', which it did, in a massacre lasting several days. Although a mild Social Democrat formally headed its government after the army's intervention, Bavaria was the first part of Germany in which the Right regained power.

Elsewhere in Germany parliamentary democracy seemed to be growing stronger. The newly elected Constituent Assembly met in Weimar and legitimated Ebert in his office. A new coalition government was formed, based on the strongest parties in the Assembly—the Social Democrats, the Zentrum, and the Democrats, an enlarged successor party to the pre-war Progressives. Only the USPD and the decimated Right were in opposition. The wheel had turned full circle. The fighting in Berlin and Munich had dashed all prospect of red revolution; the elections had not given a mandate for Socialism. The

Government looked much like the Government of Max of Baden. But the civil war between the two wings of the Labour movement saddled German democracy with a liability from which it did not recover. The SPD was blamed for the deaths of the heroes of the Revolution, for losing nerve at the vital moment, for permitting the survival of Imperial institutions, economic privilege, and anti-democratic officials. What had gone wrong?

Not only the war but the years before had shown that the SPD was the party of democratic republicanism, not of the dictatorship of the proletariat. 'We cannot say we "made" the revolution,' one of the SPD leaders reflected in retrospect, 'but we were not its opponents. . . . What is certain is that it was we who, day by day, provided the working class with aims and direction.' Yet 'aim' and 'direction' were invariably in the direction of restraint. At any given moment there were excellent tactical reasons for this. The army officers were needed, first to bring home the troops, then to maintain order, then to protect the eastern frontiers against marauders. So they retained their command. The landowners were needed to see Germany through the hungry winter, especially since the Allied blockade had not yet been lifted. So they retained their estates. The industrialists were needed to keep production going, and there was a feeling that nationalized property would be more vulnerable to Allied reparation demands than private property. So the capitalists were not expropriated. Civil servants and judges held legally guaranteed posts. To replace them with 'politically reliable' officials would be arbitrary and would reduce the morale of those who remained in service. So democratically elected governments had to rely on administrators who had been trained to serve an abstract, timeless authoritarian state—the *Obrigkeitsstaat*—and who were intellectually and emotionally out of sympathy with republican methods. Having to cope with half a dozen emergencies at once, the Government was apt to congratulate itself on keeping civilized life going at all. The winter of 1918–19 was not the time to initiate grandiose reforms: a law establishing the eight-hour working day was its principal measure. Above all there was the fear that anything resembling 'Bolshevism'—a concept generously interpreted by the Liberal and Conservative statesmen who led the victorious powers—would bring Allied military intervention.

So, while these omissions were individually defensible, their combined effect was fatal to the Republic's chances. When the revolutionary fervour subsided, the new Germany looked remarkably like the old. The Emperor was gone, but the Imperial institutions, run by men with Imperial mentalities, remained. Perhaps the provisional Government could have recruited a republican militia to keep the wilder extremists in check; perhaps some socialization of industry or land redistribution need not have led to production crises. But the Social Democratic ministers were not only extremely legalistic, observing the constitutional niceties which their enemies to the Left and Right ignored and despised, they also suffered from an inferiority complex. Condemned to opposition until 1918, largely self-educated and excluded from the higher reaches of society, they lacked—or thought they lacked—the ability to run the complex industrial and administrative machinery of Germany single-handedly. The example of Russia, where such an attempt had been made, was not encouraging.

The last two considerations form the most plausible explanation why the Revolution stalled. Modern industrial societies are complex organisms that do not lend themselves to the complete and violent overthrow of the *status quo*. By 1918 ordered life in Germany was as dependent on the division of labour, on functional specialization and sophisticated public administration as in any country in the world. Workers and peasants were as dependent on their smooth operation as generals, civil servants, and industrial managers. One and all, they would be losers from chaos. All previous revolutions, those of the American colonies, in France, or in Russia had happened in pre-industrial societies in which large parts of the population could survive on the basis of self-sufficiency while the new order replaced the old. These conditions did not apply to the German Empire in its dying days. But there was a political as well as an economic inhibiting factor. Unlike the *sans-culottes* of 1789 and the *muzhiks* of 1917, German workers were not without rights. The universal male suffrage for the Reichstag, limited though it was in its effectiveness, frustrating though it was in its denial of popular sovereignty, had accustomed all Germans to a right in political participation. To have listened to the shop stewards' and Spartacists' cry of 'all power to the councils', to have agreed to the dictatorship of the proletariat, would have led to a diminution of existing political rights. The Revolution of 1918 happened because the Imperial constitution no longer corresponded with the needs of a literate, skilled population, and had permitted an unaccountable elite to lead Germany into a war that it lost with disastrous consequences. A significant minority of the German people were, for the time being, undoubtedly seized with utopian hopes. The majority wanted something more limited: the removal of specific injustices that had already been present and visible before 1914, but that the war had rendered intolerable.

5 The Weimar Republic, 1919–1933

Democracy . . . is not only the consequence of the political and
social development of the modern state, but the only means of
directing the inverse class domination, the dictatorship of the
proletariat, into the path of a sound and just state structure, and
of salvaging the healthy core of a state-sustaining Socialism.
Salvation lies with it, and in an honest comprehension and recognition of it. We *must* learn to operate this political form and above
all gain the will to embrace it.

But that naturally implies a fundamental change, . . . above all
in our intellectual attitude towards state and society. All this
signifies the thorough recognition of a severe defeat, which imposes on us an assimilation to the rest of the political world.

(Ernst Troeltsch, *Die deutsche Demokratie*, 29 December 1918)

Our formalistic democracy has shamefully surrendered not only
to the superior material force of the enemy, but to the ideas of the
West.

(Max Hildebert Boehm, *Der Ruf der Jungen* (*The Call of
the Young*), 1921)

The Peace and the Constitution

On 31 July 1919 the Constituent Assembly in the National Theatre
completed its work. Its five months' deliberations were devoted to two
tasks, neither of which endeared it to its fellow countrymen. It accepted the terms of the Paris Peace Conference, and it drew up a
democratic, republican constitution.

The peace demands of the Allied powers, which were submitted
to the German delegation on 1 May, came as a great shock. Though
there was no specific mention of President Wilson's Fourteen Points
when the armistice was signed, politicians and public alike had

expected the peace treaty to be couched in terms of Wilsonian reconciliation. At least one of Wilson's principles had already been breached: the discussions among the victors' delegations were held behind closed doors. 'Few negotiations in history', wrote one of the participants, Sir Harold Nicolson, 'have been so secret, or indeed so occult'. The outcome of these negotiations, though it watered down many of the original demands of France and even Britain, was essentially designed to protect French security.

Overseas Germany lost all her colonies. In the West she predictably lost Alsace-Lorraine to France; less predictably she lost the Saar coal basin to France for fifteen years. In the East the German city of Memel went to Lithuania, and the German city of Danzig was made Poland's main port, under League of Nations supervision. Danzig was joined to the rest of Poland by a 'corridor' which split East Prussia from the rest of Germany. Upper Silesia, industrially rich and with a 60 per cent Polish population, was also to go to Poland. The Republic of Austria, which contained most of the German-speaking citizens of the now-defunct Habsburg Empire, was prohibited from joining the *Reich*, despite the expressed wish of the population to do so. Only on Upper Silesia did the Germans gain a concession. Supported by Lloyd George, the British Prime Minister, who wanted to prevent the creation of 'new Alsace-Lorraines', they secured a plebiscite, the outcome of which saved some of the province for Germany.

These territorial changes deprived Germany of 13 per cent of her pre-war population, 26 per cent of her coal resources, and 75 per cent of her iron ore. But this was nothing compared with the direct economic deprivations which the treaty imposed. Germany forfeited most of her overseas investments and merchant fleet; most seriously, Germany was to be required to make good all civilian damage caused to the Allied governments and their citizens. The damage was interpreted to include war pensions, mainly so that Britain could benefit more from the payments. It was not calculated at a fixed sum, but at a level to be assessed later by a commission. The imposition was justified in article 231 of the treaty, the famous 'war guilt' clause, which held that the war had been 'imposed . . . by the aggression of Germany and her allies'.

In addition most of the German battle fleet was to be surrendered, and the instrument which Tirpitz had conceived to coerce
Britain and which had seen the outbreak of the Revolution was scut-
tled at Scapa Flow on 22 June. The German army was reduced to
100,000 men. As a guarantee of the victors' security, Allied troops
were to occupy the Rhineland for fifteen years, and even after their
withdrawal the area was to remain unfortified.

When these conditions became known, the German Foreign
Minister, Count Brockdorff-Rantzau, refused to sign, and the Chancellor, the Social Democrat Scheidemann, resigned in protest at its
injustice. There were agonized debates in the National Assembly,
though it was obvious from the start that any renegotiation was out of
the question, and that rejection of the terms would bring unmitigated
disaster. In the end, against the votes of the Right and some Government supporters, the Assembly bowed to the inevitable and on 28 June
three ministers of the new Government signed on Germany's behalf.
The ceremony took place in the same hall at Versailles in which the
Empire had been proclaimed forty-eight years earlier.

With this vote and this signature another dangerous rift appeared in German public opinion. Dismay and indignation were widespread and genuine, and they were made worse by the 'war guilt'
clause, which the Allies had thought of less as a final historical judg-
ment than as legalistic underpinning for the reparations demands.
Outside Germany, the protests gained little sympathy, at any rate
initially. The treaties which Germany had imposed on defeated Russia
and Romania were infinitely harsher, and German war loans had
been raised with the assurance from the banker Karl Helfferich
that 'Der Feind wird zahlen' ('The enemy will pay'). Britain, France,
and America had done nothing to Germany that Germany would
not have done to them, given the chance. Dissenters from this
view were at first the exception. John Maynard Keynes argued in
The Economic Consequences of the Peace that to impoverish Germany
was to impoverish Europe. Some Liberals and Socialists in Britain
and France argued that the Germans who were being punished
were not the Germans who were guilty. But it was a decade or
more before this attitude became widespread, and then to the

benefit of a new set of German leaders, whose sole thought was revenge.

Inside Germany the peace terms were seen as the logical consequence of the armistice: the 'November criminals' who had signed the first now compounded their treason. Those who had every reason to hate the new political order could use the peace terms to convince their public of one vast conspiracy of subversion. Germany, they claimed, had not been militarily defeated, but politically undermined. 'What the enemy, in years of struggle, did not achieve we have done to ourselves. We thrust a dagger into the back of our fighting troops,' wrote the Conservative *Kreuzzeitung*. The German army had died, according to one Nationalist spokesman, like Siegfried: 'and the spear that was thrust by Hagen into Siegfried's body from the rear was forged a long time before'. And so the *Dolchstoßlegende*, the myth of the stab in the back, was born. In part the Republican politicians, the victims of this myth, weakened their own position. They could have admitted the war guilt of the Imperial Government, while disclaiming responsibility for its acts. This might have cut no ice diplomatically, but it would have given them the initiative domestically. As it was, fearing that admissions of guilt would aggravate the Allies' conditions, they defended Germany's part in the 1914 crisis and thereby revealed themselves as the ineffectual guardians of an innocence they claimed to believe in.

The trouble with the treaty was that it was neither conciliatory nor Carthaginian. The democratization of German government had been one of the conditions of the armistice; now the leaders of German democracy were saddled with the odium of collecting dues which they thought unjustly and arbitrarily imposed. The revision of the 'imposed peace', the 'Diktat von Versailles' became the declared objective of all parties: to outbid the moderate parties in revisionism was a heaven-sent weapon to those whose primary aim was to undermine parliamentary government.

The Republican constitution, which the National Assembly had virtually drawn up by the time the treaty was signed, also served to intensify the divisions in public opinion. The document was a model of republican sanity. It confirmed the reforms of the autumn of 1918, making the Government answerable to parliament; it confirmed the electoral law for the Constituent Assembly which gave the vote to men and women over twenty for both the Reichstag and the state parliaments. Their votes were distributed to the parties by strict proportional representation. The new constitution, however, was designed to do more than regulate the institutions of government; it was to proclaim a new political order. Unlike the Imperial constitution, but like the abortive draft of 1849, it contained a long catalogue of basic rights. These enumerated not only the rights of the citizen, such as equality before the law and freedom of speech, but the rights and empowerments attributable to the social order. The relevant articles guaranteed the rights of property and of inheritance, the freedom to engage in trade and industry, freedom of association and the protection of labour, freedom of conscience and the protection of marriage and the family. These detailed provisions indicated what had and what had not been changed by the upheavals of the previous nine months. The Weimar state was a liberal republic with extensive social provisions. All the political inequalities that had characterized the Empire were swept away. But the inherited social order was in many respects reinforced, with the constitutional guarantee of property, the family, and religious worship.

On other points, involving traditional *Reich* institutions, there were clashes among the constitution-makers. The 1848 republican flag—black, red, and gold, which is also the flag of the post-1949 Federal Republic—won narrowly over the Imperial colours. The head of state, the *Reichspräsident*, was to be elected by universal suffrage, an *Ersatzkaiser* who was to stand out among the run-of-the-mill politicians, though Ebert himself was confirmed in his office as first Republican President by the Constituent Assembly. Under article 48 the President was given powers to rule by emergency decree. He also had the right to submit parliamentary legislation to a referendum and to dissolve the Reichstag. What use he would make of these powers depended partly on the personality of the incumbent, but even more on the effectiveness of the remaining institutions. Against a stable government resting on a secure Reichstag majority, the President could do little. He was a potential counterweight only against a fragmented parliament and a weak government. Since for much of the Republic's short life the latter conditions applied, he became increasingly a force for the exercise of authoritarian and unaccountable power. Lastly, although there were strong arguments for abolishing the old Prussian state and unifying the Republic's administration, traditionalism and vested political interests secured the survival of the old *Länder*, subject only to some boundary adjustments. The upheavals of the post-war months made many people unwilling to entrust a virtual monopoly of power to Berlin. Though the Reichstag was now much the stronger of the two houses of parliament, in particular through the sole right to determine taxation, the *Länder* managed to retain control of two important and controversial matters, public order and education.

Whatever prestige republicanism and parliamentary democracy might have enjoyed at the time of the Empire's collapse—if only as a defence against revolution—had greatly diminished a year later. Social unrest and the weakening of authority made many people yearn for the certainties of Imperial days. The men of Weimar were seen as the men of Versailles: the constitution and the treaty were both seen as embodying alien principles, imposed on Germany by the victorious West. There was an opposite disenchantment on the part of many of the workers who had hoped, if not for revolution, at least for radical reform and now saw, as a consequence of the maintenance of 'order', a social structure differing little from that of 1914 or 1890.

These disillusionments were mirrored in the first Reichstag election of June 1920. The 'Weimar' coalition which had governed for over a year and held the political initiative since the Peace Resolution of 1917 lost its majority and never again regained it. The SPD lost nearly half its support, much of it to the USPD. The Catholic vote held steady, but the Conservative, Bavarian wing of the Zentrum broke away to form an independent party, less willing to support the Republic. The most disastrous losses were those of the Democrats (DDP), the party *par excellence* of parliamentary Liberalism and the Weimar constitution. They lost three-fifths of their support; at their expense the Right swelled. The chief gainers were the Democrats' rivals, the People's Party (DVP), led by the ex-National Liberal Gustav Stresemann, whose loyalty to the Republic was at this stage dubious; and the Nationalists (DNVP), reconstituted from old Conservatives and pan-Germanists who were frankly anti-Republican and anti-democratic and who secured what had always eluded the old Junker-led Conservative Party, a firm urban base in the western parts of the country.

These developments underlined how divisive an event the collapse and Revolution of 1918 had been. On the one hand the conduct of the war, and the hardships associated with it, had undermined faith not only in the Imperial Government, the army, and the dynasty, but in all authority, a loss that any new regime would find it difficult to recover from. With the collapse of the Empire, three ultimately irreconcilable political tendencies emerged. The first comprised those who resented all democratization and any loss of their political or social privileges. Initially they were isolated and decided to lie low, but before long they recovered their confidence and exercised increasing influence on the politics of the Republic. At the other extreme were the revolutionaries, who hoped not only for political democracy, but the abolition of capitalism. Utopian enthusiasm is difficult to sustain, and support for a revolution fluctuated wildly, subsiding after the crushing of the Berlin rising in 1919, but reviving, as we shall see, in the spring of 1920. Between these two forces were those politicians and social groups for whom the avoidance of chaos was the primary concern. In an advanced industrial state like Germany, dependent on the smooth running of services and with a long tradition of effective administration, challenged in 1918–19 by military defeat, a blockade, and the task of demobilizing millions of soldiers, the maintenance of a functioning state apparatus was a matter of obvious urgency.

The economic expectations of the revolutionaries were, moreover, illusory. The war had impoverished Germany; reparations and the loss of territory would impoverish her further. It was not until 1928 that the gross domestic product would reach pre-war levels. No political party was challenged more severely by these dilemmas than the apparent victors of the fall of the Empire, the Social Democrats. Overnight they were required to assume governmental responsibility, to govern in coalition with non-Socialist parties, to ensure law and order, to decide which of their long-term aims were to be postponed or even abandoned. Under these circumstances a split in the SPD and a division in the working-class movement would almost certainly have been unavoidable, even if it had not already happened in 1917. What made this split fatal for Weimar democracy was its depth, and the intensity of the hatred between the SPD and its chief rival on the Left, the KPD. The SPD's insistence on crushing any radicalism of the Left, if necessary by calling on the forces of the Right, created resentments that made even tactical co-operation between the two wings of the Labour movement impossible; it also almost certainly strengthened the KPD, which at no stage had an interest in defending parliamentary democracy, at the expense of the SPD.

The Weimar Republic was further weakened by a parallel polarization on the Right. The terms of the Versailles Treaty gave the first major impetus to the politics of resentment; the taxation plans of Matthias Erzberger, the Zentrum Finance Minister, gave the second. The burden of the war loans, the weakening of the post-war economy, and the demands of reparations all pointed to an increased tax-collecting role for the *Reich* Government. Erzberger's principal measures were a *Reich* income tax, something that no Imperial government had been able to enact, and an Emergency Capital Levy, payable in instalments. This policy aroused the hostility of all those Conservatives who believed in states' rights and regarded all central government as by definition spendthrift; all those who saw the tax reform as an attack on property; and all those to whom Erzberger was already a *bête noire*, given his role in the Peace Resolution and the acceptance of the Treaty. Nothing was therefore easier than to turn opposition to the tax reform into an attack on the Republic.

This shift from the political middle towards the extremes, and particularly towards the Right, was reflected in the colouring of the Republic's later governments. The USPD was too isolated to think of participating or to be asked to do so. So, *a fortiori*, were the Communists, who inherited most of their voters after the USPD decided on self-dissolution in 1922. The Social Democrats withdrew from the cabinet in August 1920 and, except for two brief periods of office under non-Socialist Chancellors, did not return to power until they formed the Great Coalition in 1928. Defeated on the battlefield, defeated at the conference table, defeated at the polls, the Republic embarked on its uncertain career.

Survival and Revival

For the first three years the new state led a hand-to-mouth existence, as it slowly established its legitimacy in the eyes of the population. The challenges came from extremist opponents of parliamentary republicanism, from the victor powers, and from the constituent *Länder*. Even before the 1920 election there had been an attempt at a right-wing *coup d'état* which ought to have raised Republican morale but, typically, failed to do so. The *putsch* was led by a former Prussian civil servant, Wolfgang Kapp, and the commander of the Berlin army district, General Walther Freiherr von Lüttwitz. The Government was obliged to retire to Stuttgart, but the *putsch* fizzled out. While many army officers and civil servants, and some politicians, such as Stresemann and the DNVP, sympathized with its aims, few were prepared to risk their political future on so half-baked an adventure. The *putsch* was defeated, first by a general strike, called by all the unions, which paralysed Berlin; secondly by the strange neutrality of the army. The army's clear duty was to support the legal Government: this, in the words of General Hans von Seeckt to the Minister of Defence, it was not prepared to do.

Troops do not fire on troops. Do you, Herr Minister, perhaps have the intention of tolerating a battle in front of the Brandenburg Gate among troops who have only just fought side by side against the enemy?

How dependent the Government was on the army's benevolent neutrality was shown in the next few weeks. In some areas, particularly the Ruhr, the anti-Kapp strike movement began to assume revolutionary proportions. For a time it looked as though the radicalism of the winter of 1918–19 had returned. To dislodge the 'Red' militias from the industrial towns the army was needed and the army, in turn, needed the *Freikorps*, who had but recently supported the Kapp–Lüttwitz adventure. The renewed threat from the Left expunged the discredit of the Right.

Nor did other acts of right-wing terrorism leave lasting impressions, however great the momentary indignation they evoked. In 1921 one of the leaders of the Zentrum, Matthias Erzberger, inspirer of the Reichstag Peace Resolution and a signatory of the armistice and the peace treaty, was murdered. A year later, the Foreign Minister, Walther Rathenau, especially vulnerable as a Jew, was murdered. In each case the assassins belonged to the Erhardt Brigade, implicated in the Kapp *putsch*. The assassination of Rathenau caused a particularly unfavourable impression abroad, and the Chancellor, Josef Wirth of the Zentrum, declared before the Reichstag: 'There the enemy stands, where Mephisto drips his poison into a nation's wounds. . . . That enemy stands on the right.'

Neither then nor later could any statesman convince the German people of this truth. The real Mephistopheles they saw in the vindictive Western powers who sought to enslave Germany, the baneful bond of blood between their demands and the pragmatic Weimar politicians who saw no alternative but a 'policy of fulfilment'. The predominant mood of Germany was one of national resentment and anyone who articulated this mood, whatever his faults of style, could gain a more indulgent hearing than any *Verzichtspolitiker* or 'defeatist politician'. In this demagogic competition the anti-republican Right had a clear advantage, though some of the Left, in particular the Communists, were not far behind in equating Western policies with an imperialist rivalry for which all classes in Germany paid the bill.

The resentment was heightened by the reparations terms which the Allied commission presented in April 1921: a non-negotiable demand for 132 thousand million gold marks (just over 30,000 million dollars). Wirth, Rathenau, and the Social Democrats who supported them decided that Germany should put the best possible face on the inevitable, and pursue a 'fulfilment' line, but such was the weakness of the German economy that even the first instalment of deliveries was not handed over in time. While opinion in Britain was swinging over to concessions towards Germany, a hard-line government in France, under Raymond Poincaré, insisted on exacting the full quota. Following up an ultimatum, French and Belgian troops moved over the line of the Rhineland occupation zone in January 1923 and occupied the Ruhr industrial area to enforce deliveries—an occupation which was to last ten months.

The main cause of Germany's economic feebleness was the creeping inflation which the war had initiated and which the Government failed to halt thereafter. In one way the escalating inflation had its causes even before 1914, when, as we have seen, the Imperial Government experienced difficulties in covering its costs. It was aggravated by the policy of financing the war by loans rather than, as in Britain, by taxation and by the drop in tax receipts after the end of the war. Weimar was, in the words of the historian of its inflation, Gerald Feldman, a mortgaged republic. At the beginning of the reparations crisis a paper mark was worth one-hundredth of a pre-war gold mark. The hyper-inflation, which began in April 1923, left the mark, at the end, with two-thousand-millionths of its 1914 value.

Inflations have political causes and require political cures. The reasons for the long-drawn-out German inflation and its disastrous climax are complex. They were aggravated by the weakness of post-1918 governments, the veto power of domestic interest groups, and the entanglement with reparations. In the immediate aftermath of the war, no German government had the strength and the authority to demand the sacrifices that would have stifled the inflationary pressures. In Britain the Lloyd George Government, buttressed by a landslide electoral majority and the bonus of military victory, had no compunction at raising interest rates and accepting the odium of unemployment. Nor did United States administrations hesitate to defeat labour union demands. No German government could throttle the incipient economic recovery in this way, or offend the newly euphoric Labour movement, whose militancy was enhanced first by the Revolution and then by the post-Kapp strikes. Indeed, the first stage of the post-war inflation, by cheapening credit, stimulated investment and eased the reversion to a peacetime economy. True, it devalued the exchange rate of the Reichsmark and thereby encouraged a flight of capital abroad. But this devaluation also brought its short-term benefits, by cheapening German exports. Thus business had some vested interest in a lax fiscal policy, which aided expansion; labour had little inclination to give up its newly won bargaining power and shorter working week; and the Government, while perennially short of revenue, could see inflation eroding its burden of debt. Nor was it politically easy to call on the population to tighten its belt while speculators and war profiteers continued to flaunt their wealth.

The final blow to any political will that successive governments might have had to throttle inflation was the reparations bill. The inflation was not a direct means of evading reparations payments; the reparations were denominated in gold. But it was a bargaining counter. German negotiators argued that the reparations burden weakened the economy and the currency; it increased the cost of gold to Germany and made it more difficult for governments to stem inflation. They therefore demanded that the Allies ease the burden as a condition for stabilizing the Reichsmark. The demand fell on deaf ears. The Allies insisted that the causes of the German inflation were purely domestic and that its cure was a German domestic problem.

It was this deadlock that brought about the Ruhr occupation and it was under the occupation that the final twist in the inflationary spiral began, as the markets inside and outside Germany lost all confidence in the Reichsmark. The Government tried to undermine the occupation by ordering a policy of 'passive resistance'. Since this amounted to no more than administrative non-co-operation, and since the objectives of the occupation could be largely achieved without the co-operation of the Germans, it was little more than a solemn farce. Reparations and the Ruhr occupation aggravated the inflation, but had not created it. But many Germans, especially pauperized bourgeois Germans, saw a direct causal link; the dual experience embittered many who were already inclined to blame the Republic for all their ills and made them even readier to listen to nationalist agitators.

During 1923 the Republic was further weakened by a number of challenges to its authority which, though facilitated by the Ruhr-inflation crisis, arose basically out of the structural weaknesses of the Republic and the absence of a political consensus. One of the weaknesses was that the ideological diversity of the country became institutionalized in various *Land* governments, the parties acting much like new dynasties. In Prussia, which the constitution-makers had, on second thoughts, preserved intact, this was a source of strength to the regime. Here, thanks to universal suffrage, the Social Democrats and Zentrum now predominated, and for most of the Republic's lifetime 'Weimar coalitions' headed the Prussian Government. Since Prussia had the responsibility for public order in Berlin, control of the Prussian police was a politically highly sensitive matter.

Elsewhere the vestiges of federalism were less helpful, least of all in Bavaria. Here the restoration of the Right, which dated from the overthrow of the Munich Soviet Republic, was confirmed after the Kapp *putsch*, with the appointment of Gustav von Kahr, a high official with monarchist leanings, as Prime Minister. The traditional conservatism of Bavaria was accentuated by experience of the brief left-wing adventure. Officials, police officers, and judges were overwhelmingly unfavourable to the Republic. They protected the various armed bands—*Freikorps, Einwohnerwehr, Vaterländische Verbände*—which meted out indiscriminate political justice, and offered hospitality to those that were chased out of other parts of the country. When the chief of the Munich police, Ernst Pöhner, was asked about these gangs, he replied that there were not enough of them. Wilhelm Frick and Josef Gürtner, later Hitler's Ministers of the Interior and of Justice, served on Pöhner's staff.

One of the many nationalist groupings that flourished here was the Deutsche Arbeiterpartei, founded by a Munich railwayman, Anton Drexler, but soon under the dictatorial control of one of its early recruits, an out-of-work ex-serviceman with exceptional oratorical gifts, Adolf Hitler. His ability to organize, and above all to raise funds, made his party, renamed the Nationalsozialistische Deutsche Arbeiterpartei (NSDAP: 'Nazi'), one of the biggest of its kind, although still restricted to Bavaria. Another characteristic of the party was its strong-arm squad, the Schutz-Abteilung (SA), organized by a Bavarian regular officer, Major Ernst Röhm, from among his *Freikorps* companions. Its nominal task was to protect speakers at the party's meetings; its *raison d'être* to pick fights with opponents.

The first major clash between Bavaria and the *Reich* concerned these private armies. At the time when the Versailles Treaty came into effect, and the whole German army was not supposed to exceed 100,000 men, there were reckoned to be at least 420,000 armed irregulars in Bavaria alone. Only after the murder of Erzberger was it possible to enforce some disbandment. A more serious act of insubordination occurred during the Ruhr crisis when, in August 1923, Gustav Stresemann formed a government, including Social Democrats, to secure French withdrawal by abandoning passive resistance. In response to this left-wing challenge Kahr was appointed Government commissioner with dictatorial powers. More seriously, the Bavarian contingents of the army, under General Otto von Lossow, pledged their support to him. Bavaria was therefore in virtual rebellion and there was talk of a march on Berlin. This seemed to Hitler to be the opportunity he had been waiting for, especially as he had secured respectability through the support of General Ludendorff. On 8 November he and some followers burst into a meeting in a large Munich beer-cellar, the *Bürgerbräu*, addressed by Kahr, and persuaded the Bavarian dictator to engage in a joint *putsch*. The morning after, Kahr and Lossow thought better of it, and only Hitler and Ludendorff marched to the city centre with a band of followers, where they were easily dispersed and arrested.

Apart from their hatred of democracy and internationalism Kahr and Hitler had little in common. The Bavarian Government was ultra-Conservative; it wanted a restoration of the monarchy and the old *Reich*. Hitler despised such men as has-beens. His ambition was to lead a mass movement which would establish an élitist dictatorship on racialist lines. The lesson he drew from the failure of his *putsch* was that he needed to act with, not against, the forces of order and property, and that he would have to wait until they needed him more than he needed them.

A different threat to Berlin came from the *Länder* of Saxony and Thuringia, where the Social Democrats decided to form coalitions with the Communists. Whether these two industrial states could have formed a viable base for a new wave of proletarian revolution is doubtful; in any case they did not get the opportunity. Since the existence of these Left governments was a pretext for Kahr's insubordination and intolerable to the army, a military expedition was authorized by presidential decree to overthrow them. Kahr and Ludendorff, however, got off scot-free, and even Hitler was sentenced to only five years' detention, of which he served eight months. Once more fear of the Left had put a premium on subversion from the Right.

Even before these revolts fizzled out the central government had regained the initiative. A new unit of currency, the Rentenmark, was established, to be replaced the next year by a gold-based Reichsmark. Elections in France resulted in a government of the Left, with the Radical Edouard Herriot as Prime Minister and the conciliatory Aristide Briand as Foreign Minister. This paved the way for a new relationship with the outside world. Its architect was Stresemann, who had ceased to be Chancellor but remained Foreign Minister until 1929.

The most immediate problem to be solved was that of reparations. To maintain regular payments Germany needed a stable economy and currency; to achieve these she needed a dollar loan. Both were ensured by the Dawes Plan, drawn up by an international committee under the American general, Charles Dawes. The demands that this committee made, though heavy, were realistic. In return for a loan of 800 million gold marks, which provided the backing for the new currency, Germany was to make guaranteed annual payments, the revenue for which was to come from bond issues and specially earmarked budget and railway surpluses. Half the governors of the Reichsbank would have to be foreigners. But the size of the loan was tempting enough to overcome nationalist objections: the Dawes Plan was accepted and the occupation of the Ruhr thereby ended.

Though the Dawes settlement made possible the restabilization of the German economy, the restabilization of society was less easy. Not everyone had suffered impoverishment during the inflation, and those who did suffer did not suffer equally. What the inflation had done was to create a climate of profound insecurity, the after-effects of which lasted a generation or more. With the insecurity came a further loss of social solidarity beyond that caused by the last years of the war and the upheavals of the Revolution. Suspicions and resentments between social groups were aggravated and were reflected in a growing fragmentation of the party system. Nor did the details of the stabilization satisfy all Germans. The terms on which creditors and bondholders saw their devalued assets translated into new Reichsmarks created another class of those who were potentially alienated from the Republic.

Stresemann's longer-term ambition, after securing the Dawes settlements, was to re-establish Germany's position in the international community and this again could be achieved only on terms acceptable to the West. Even before 1924 Germany had not been diplomatically isolated. The overwhelming priority which 'revision' had in the Republic's foreign policy led its statesmen to seek the support of any other revisionist power there might be. The chief candidate for any such partnership, however unlikely at first sight, was

Soviet Russia. Lenin's peace policy in 1917 had been 'no annexations, no indemnities': Versailles was in clear contradiction to this formula and Russia did not hesitate to denounce the 'robber treaties'. Moreover the victorious powers had done all they could to undermine the Bolshevik regime, to the extent of sending expeditionary forces during the civil war which followed the Revolution. The territorial resettlement of Eastern Europe displeased Russia as much as Germany. Deprived of Russia as her eastern 'anchor', France encouraged the establishment of a large Poland, with whom she signed a treaty of alliance in 1921. France also did all she could to ensure generous frontiers for the succession states of the Habsburg Monarchy—Czechoslovakia, Romania, and Yugoslavia—and these, known as the 'Little Entente', were also heavily dependent on French diplomatic patronage, thus forming a strong anti-revisionist bloc.

Thus the 1922 Treaty of Rapallo between Germany and Russia ought not to have created the shock and surprise in the rest of Europe which it did. It was not a military alliance, but Germany became the first capitalist state to break the diplomatic quarantine of Russia, and both states ostentatiously agreed to waive any wartime claims on each other. The political colouring of the Soviet regime notwithstanding, Rapallo was welcomed by the German Right—by industry for the opportunities in trade that the treaty opened, by the army for the facilities which were secretly agreed for the production of arms and the training of men beyond the Versailles limits, by all for the added weight it gave to any defiance of the peace treaty.

Stresemann's 'turn to the West' in 1924 was therefore more welcome to the Republican parties than to the opposition of Right and Left. The crowning outcome of his initiative was the Locarno Treaties. Germany abandoned all revisionist claims in the west (which meant principally Alsace-Lorraine) and the security of the frontier was guaranteed by Britain and Italy as well as the neighbours involved. In return Germany was admitted to the League of Nations (also anathema to Communists and Nationalists). But Stresemann also secured valuable concessions. Germany was exempted from taking part in any military operations that might be ordered by the League, and thus kept on good terms with Russia. A treaty dealing with Germany's eastern frontiers was much vaguer than the 'western' Locarno: it merely provided for arbitration in case of dispute and it was not signed by Britain, who had no desire to underwrite these French spheres of influence. Thus Stresemann gave away nothing in the East and did nothing to stop the secret rearmament, of which he was well aware. What he did, and what the collapse of Poincaré's pound-of-flesh policies enabled him to do, was to make Germany a normal member of the diplomatic community. As a sign of their reborn confidence in Germany the Western powers soon abandoned any effective control of German armaments and prematurely withdrew their last occupation troops from the right bank of the Rhine.

The era of Stresemann was the high noon of the Weimar Republic. Tempers dropped, political extremism subsided. In large part this was due to the return of prosperity. Between 1924 (admittedly a very bad year) and 1928 money wages doubled and the value of the currency was maintained. The standard of living was higher in 1928 than in 1913. Unemployment was generally below one million. In 1927 the expansion of the German welfare state culminated in the introduction of a comprehensive unemployment insurance scheme. German industry regained its technical and organizational lead. The Dawes loan, following the premium which the inflation had put on machines and bricks and mortar, encouraged modernization. The trend towards vast combines, already in evidence before 1914, was accelerated. The four major chemical firms fused in the I. G. Farben, which in turn reached pricing and marketing agreements with its principal British and American equivalents. The six major steel concerns fused in the Vereinigte Stahlwerke. Though these developments helped German manufactures in the world's markets, they did not necessarily strengthen the Republic politically.

Men like Dr Carl Duisberg of I. G. Farben, Albert Vögler of the steel combine, and Alfred Hugenberg, the general manager of Krupp's, regarded the Republic with distaste, if not hostility. They were certainly more powerful men than any Chancellor or President. Their stake was so vast, the patents they possessed often so vital strategically, that they considered themselves entitled to negotiate independently with the administration, with the army, and with the intelligence services—ambitions which the Third Reich was better able to satisfy than the Weimar Republic.

Nor can the Republic's political leaders be said to have made the most of their opportunities during the mid-1920s. The notion that political parties should train men of ministerial calibre and accept responsibility for overall policy was understood by too few voters or politicians. The notion that 'administration' was good and 'politics' bad, that parties served, at best, as spokesmen for sectional interests, survived from the image of the state under the Empire. The Republic's system of proportional representation perpetuated and accentuated party fragmentation, but did not cause it. The cause was the failure, during the Empire, to associate parliamentary politicians with responsibility for the welfare of the state. The 1928 elections, which gave the Republican parties the best results since 1919 and which resulted in an SPD-led Great Coalition, thus gave a misleading impression of Republican strength. The 491 seats were shared among sixteen parties, only four of whom held over 50 seats. Many of the remainder represented only the narrowest regional and occupational interests, like the Wirtschaftspartei (Economic Party) or the Bayerischer Bauernbund (Bavarian Peasant League). The fragmentation of interests that the inflation had created had evidently not been remedied. Attempts to unite the various Liberal trends in one middle-class Republican party failed; political Catholicism remained divided; and the Social Democrats were unable to widen their appeal, or to slough off their reputation for mediocrity, pedantry, and bureaucratism. Only eight of the twenty-one cabinets in the Republic's lifetime rested on secure parliamentary majorities; the rest were 'tolerated' by parties not represented in the Government. Four out of twelve Chancellors, and a similar proportion of cabinet ministers, were 'non-party experts', drawn from outside the ranks of professional politics. During periods of crisis—in 1923 and after 1930—the Reichstag abdicated altogether, leaving the Chancellor to govern by decree. In 1927 Edgar Jung, one of the most prominent Conservative theorists, later Franz von Papen's secretary and murdered by the Nazis, wrote: 'If there were to be an opinion survey, not of those who support today's Republic, but of those who love it, the result would be devastating.' The truth of his observation had been illustrated two years earlier, in the presidential election held on the death of Ebert. Field Marshal Hindenburg, nominated by the parties of the Right, defeated Wilhelm Marx of the Zentrum and the Communist Ernst Thälmann, by recruiting many who normally did not vote and some who normally voted for Republican parties. In Hindenburg a man of the old order now stood at the head of the state, a man who had closer links with the army and the landowners of the East than with the pillars of the Republic.

It was not merely industry which considered itself exempt from complete loyalty to the regime. The Churches, though they had little to complain of in their treatment by the state, remained lukewarm. The Protestant Churches looked back with nostalgia to the official position they had enjoyed under the deposed monarchs, especially in Prussia; their clergy and laity were predominantly nationalist. Like the Catholic Church they recoiled from the greater permissiveness in art, literature, and private morals which seemed to flourish under the more liberal aegis of the Republic. Catholicism was particularly conservative in Bavaria. The Archbishop of Munich, Cardinal Faulhaber, later to be harassed by the Gestapo for his link with the anti-Hitler resistance, refused to celebrate a requiem for the deceased President Ebert, who was not a practising Christian.

The civil service and judiciary continued largely to be staffed by men imbued with Imperial principles, especially since little was done to reform the educational system. Though such men claimed to serve 'the state' rather than governments, their system of values led them to interpret this code in anti-democratic terms. This came out most clearly in the uneven measure which the courts treated to acts of political violence or murder: those emanating from the Left, though less numerous, were dealt with much more harshly than those from the Right. Attempts by some governments, notably that of Prussia, to appoint men in sympathy with newer policies were resented as political interference and merely alienated professional civil servants further from the Republic.

That the army possessed all these characteristics in an extreme form is evident from the high-handed way in which it interpreted its duties whenever it might be needed. The new *Reichswehr* was largely the work of General Hans von Seeckt, who was its commander from 1920 to 1926. He turned the numerical restrictions of the Versailles Treaty to his advantage, using it to recruit much more selectively than had been possible before the war. The proportion of aristocrats among officers was higher in the mid-1920s than in 1913; the non-commissioned ranks were filled with highly trained, politically 'reliable' men who could handle much larger numbers when this once more became possible. The army's solidarity and independence was well illustrated at the time of the Bavarian crisis in 1923. When Ebert asked Seeckt where the army stood, Seeckt replied, with pride as well as accuracy, 'The army stands behind me'.

It was symptomatic of this situation that the Republic never gained the whole-hearted support of the academic and intellectual community. Of writers in the front rank only Gerhart Hauptmann and Thomas Mann—the latter a late convert—were truly committed to it. *Der Zauberberg* must rank as a more moving and revealing epic than many longer-lasting or more successful regimes can claim to be remembered by. Distinguished scholars—the sociologist Max Weber, the theologian Ernst Troeltsch, the historian Friedrich Meinecke—rallied more out of common sense or duty than enthusiasm. They were 'Vernunftsrepublikaner' (Republicans of the head), but 'Herzensmonarchisten' (monarchists of the heart). Others on the Left—dramatists like Ernst Toller and Bertolt Brecht, artists like George Grosz and Käthe Kollwitz—were too concerned to expose the hypocrisies of bourgeois society to be the Republic's allies against their joint enemies.

To most Germans, articulate and inarticulate, the energy, the experimentation, the chaotic creativity which made Weimar culture the envy and Mecca of so many foreigners represented *Kulturbolschewismus*, the overturning of forms and values in a world in which too much had been overturned already. The predominant cry was in favour of what Hugo von Hofmannsthal, in a lecture delivered in 1927 at the University of Munich, called 'a Conservative revolution'. The denial of materialism and egalitarianism, the revival of hierarchy and national consciousness, the praise of tradition and rural civilization, separation from the economically and politically victorious West—these were the common themes of such otherwise divergent manifestos as Count Hermann Keyserling's *Reisetagebuch eines Philosophen* (*The Travel Diary of a Philosopher*), Oswald Spengler's

Untergang des Abendlandes (*The Decline of the West*), and Arthur Moeller von den Bruck's *Das dritte Reich* (*The Third Reich*). Much more even than before 1914, youth listened to this romantic message and flocked to the *Bünde*, some of them merely escapist, others aggressively reactionary, that made up the Youth Movement.

The Rise of Hitler

The stability of the Stresemann years rested on economic prosperity; this in turn depended on world trends, and particularly on trends in the USA, given the role of American loans in Germany's recovery. By the end of 1929 a distinct deterioration had set in. In October Stresemann died: his death removed not only the architect of Germany's diplomatic comeback but the one major representative of the conservative middle classes committed to the Republic. In the same month began the collapse of share prices on the New York Stock Exchange, putting at risk the many short-term loans on deposit in Germany. Yet even before the autumn of 1929 there had been warnings that good times could not last. The decline in the German economy had begun in 1928, partly because the overheated American boom neutralized the attractiveness of investment in Germany, which had been one of the features of the Dawes Plan. Indeed, by the spring of 1929 it had become necessary to rephase Germany's reparations payments through the Young Plan.

Unlike the Dawes and any previous reparations settlement, it named a total sum. Germany's remaining liability was put at 120,000 million marks (28,000 million dollars), to be repaid over fifty-nine years. This was a much lower annual rate than before and a much lower sum than the Allies had originally reckoned with; its political effect was nevertheless disastrous. By spelling out, for the first time, how much, and for how long, Germany would be indebted, it helped to rouse opinion against the treaties, and to revive agitation from the extreme Right. In the 1928 elections the right-wing opposition—both Nationalist and Nazi—had done badly. The intransigent wing of the DNVP attributed this defeat to their participation in Republican

governments; their spokesman, Alfred Hugenberg, who had gradu-
ated from managing the Krupp empire to control of the Scherl news-
paper combine and the Ufa film corporation, became party chairman.
The Young Plan gave him his opportunity to create a broadly
based, nationalist, anti-Republican political movement. He launched a
petition to demand a referendum that would repudiate the Young Plan
in particular, and the Treaty of Versailles in general. He did so in
company with the ex-servicemen's organization Stahlhelm, which had
strong links with the DNVP; the Pan-German League; and Adolf
Hitler. The petition gained four million signatures, the referendum
just under six million votes—nothing like enough for success, but an
extremely valuable publicity exercise. What was significant about
Hugenberg's new alignment was that it drew in the Nazi Party.

Since his release from prison in 1924, Hitler had ranked as little
more than a sectarian fanatic. The party was low in funds and threatened by splits. The original programme, the 'unalterable' Twenty-
Five Points, had contained a strong dose of social radicalism and
anti-capitalism, above all the 'breaking of interest slavery', which was
the hobby-horse of the party's chief economist, Gottfried Feder. This
dislike of modern industrial society, and the cash basis of social relationships in it, had deep roots in the romantic anti-Semitic, *völkisch*
movement of the nineteenth century.

Hitler shared its prejudices, but did not give the social part of the
programme high priority. He himself was obsessed with a racial doctrine in which he saw the key to history, to economic life, and to
international relations. He formulated politics, in a way which had
become popular by the turn of the century, by analogy with Darwinian
biology, as a struggle for the survival of the fittest: 'The sin against
blood and race is the original sin in this world', he wrote in *Mein
Kampf*,

Völkisch ideology in no way acknowledges the equality of races,
but . . . considers it its duty, in accordance with the eternal will that commands this world, to foster the victory of the better and the stronger, the
defeat of the worse and the weaker.

There were, moreover, tactical reasons for playing down any
threats to property rights in the party's manifesto, since Hitler had

decided that he could come to power only by legal means, and only with the help of conservative Nationalists. The party's left wing was therefore either persuaded of the superiority of Hitler's tactics (Joseph Goebbels, for example) or driven into the wilderness (Otto Strasser). So the offer of Hugenberg's embrace suited Hitler admirably. Each of the partners calculated he would gain from the connection; in the nature of things only one of them could be right.

As the world economic crisis grew worse, and the Great Coalition floundered more deeply, the enemies of the Republic prospered. The Great Coalition, comprising all parties favourable to the Republic, had been formed after the moderate parties' election victory in 1928. Yet beyond an attachment to parliamentary methods the SPD, the Zentrum, the Democrats, and the DVP had little in common. On economic policy, on education, on Church–state relations they were divided. In countries accustomed to democratic stability, elections can be fought to decide between policies and governmental teams, taking for granted universal acceptance of the constitution. In Weimar Germany the choice was more often than not for or against the constitution, leaving it to multi-party coalitions to bargain about the issues which the election left unresolved. So, while the Government struggled to get the Young Plan through the Reichstag, and was deadlocked on the issue of social insurance contributions, production fell, interest rates—designed to attract the savings needed for reparations—remained high, and unemployment rose. Agriculture was, if anything, in a worse condition than industry. Technical backwardness and the fall in world food prices imposed intolerable debt burdens on many peasants. The enforced sales of family holdings led to first passive, then violent, resistance under the aegis of the *Landvolk* movement; it also gained an eager audience for the Nazi message of 'breaking interest slavery'.

The collapse of the Great Coalition in March 1930 illustrated all the weaknesses of Weimar parliamentarism. Faced with the familiar crisis of a budget deficit, the Right, represented by the DVP, rejected all thought of higher direct taxes or of an increase in contributions for unemployment insurance. The Left, represented by the SPD, insisted on a temporary property tax in return for their members' increased unemployment contributions and reduced benefits. Within the cabinet a painful compromise was reached on an economy package, but this was undone by the parliamentary parties. Within the DVP the pressure from its industrialists' wing strengthened the wish to bring the coalition to an end. Within the SPD, pressure from its left wing and above all the trade unions undermined support for the package. There was therefore no parliamentary majority for the coalition's package and the cabinet resigned on 27 March. It was the last day of the last government of the Weimar Republic that was based on a parliamentary majority.

The new Chancellor was Heinrich Brüning of the Zentrum, a Catholic lawyer, a much-decorated war veteran, and a confidant of President Hindenburg, whose views on 'strong government' he shared. Hindenburg agreed to Brüning's request to govern by decree under article 48 of the constitution, a request that he had refused to Hermann Müller, the Chancellor of the Great Coalition. He also agreed to new elections. Forces other than those of the Reichstag had helped undermine the Müller cabinet. A month before its collapse, the President of the Reichsbank, Hjalmar Schacht, had ostentatiously resigned to show his displeasure at the inadequacy of the economy measures. Hindenburg was actively working towards a government of the Right, without the SPD. Yet neither of these manœuvres would have succeeded had the Great Coalition maintained its cohesion and the parties on which it rested maintained their support for it. In that event the economic package could have been implemented, the election postponed, and the disasters that followed could—conceivably— have been avoided.

Under the impact of the crisis the 1930 elections produced a result that made parliamentary institutions virtually unworkable. The Nazi Party leapt from 12 to 107 seats. They, not the DNVP, were the beneficiaries of Hugenberg's manœuvre. Splinter parties, concerned with pressing only the narrowest of sectional interests, went up from 51 to 72 seats. The only political forces that survived this holocaust were those with firm social roots dating from the Empire—Catholicism and the working-class Left. But within the Zentrum, once the party of democrats like Wirth and Erzberger, power passed to authoritarian Conservatives like Heinrich Brüning and its new chairman, Monsignor Ludwig Kaas, disenchanted with parliamentary government. And within the Left the Communists, up from 54 to 77 seats, were gaining at the expense of the Social Democrats. But it was Hitler who now carried the main challenge to 'the system', as he liked to call it. He had become, overnight, a figure of international importance. His antagonist, Brüning, meanwhile set himself the task of solving the reparations problem, and with it the worst of the financial crisis, by a combination of domestic austerity and diplomatic bargaining.

Brüning was in power for two and a quarter years. His cabinets lacked working majorities in the Reichstag; in the last cabinet 'non-party experts' outnumbered party politicians. The Reichstag became increasingly irrelevant. It met only 41 times in 1931 and 13 times in 1932. In 1932 it passed five laws, while the President issued 59 decrees. Article 48 of the constitution, intended to cover special national emergencies, now became the normal instrument for performing the function that the legislature was unable to fulfil. In its last two years the Weimar Republic was governed in the name of the *Ersatzkaiser* by a bureaucracy whose assumptions and values were those of the Empire. The Reichstag exercised less power in 1932 than before 1914.

The measures Brüning took to remedy the crisis were courageous: in retrospect they can also be shown to have been disastrous. The main phobia of German public opinion—or at least of the conservative classes to whom Brüning, Hindenburg, and the civil service were closest—was inflation. Brüning therefore determined to balance the budget, a difficult operation since falling production and falling incomes meant lower tax revenue. Many modern economists would prescribe a budget deficit for the situation Germany faced—lower taxes, higher government expenditure, or both. Orthodoxy in 1930 demanded the opposite. The Government therefore raised taxes, reduced public investment, and cut social benefits at a time of record unemployment and ordered reductions in wages and civil service salaries. It also decided against a devaluation of the overvalued gold-based Reichsmark, because this would have been interpreted as an attempt to sabotage the Young Plan.

Brüning was determined not to repeat the mistakes of 1923. He would retain Germany's creditworthiness so as to maintain the inflow of foreign loans. He would try to end reparations by diplomacy, thus scoring a major political triumph and taking the wind out of the Nazis' sails. Neither calculation worked. Unlike the 1923 crisis, that of 1931 was world-wide. Apart from the French no-one had any credit to invest in Germany, however worthy she might be of it. Minor palliatives, like the proposed customs union with Austria, which would also appeal to nationalist opinion, were vetoed by the victor powers. In July 1931 President Herbert Hoover of the USA proposed a general moratorium on all inter-Allied war debts and reparations— one which, as it turned out, remained permanently in force; it marked the end of reparations. But because the decision came unilaterally from America and not as a direct result of German lobbying, Brüning reaped little benefit from it.

Meanwhile the German people were becoming more acutely aware of the economic crisis. By the spring of 1932 there were over six million unemployed and almost everyone's standard of living had dropped. The only interest group to get special treatment from the national exchequer was agriculture, accustomed since the 1870s to public largesse. Large subsidies, under the name of *Osthilfe*, were earmarked to relieve the East Elbian landowners of debt and mortgage burdens. Many of them simply used the money to enlarge their estates, among them the President's son, Oskar von Hindenburg. His implication in these scandals was of some political importance, given his growing ascendancy over his ageing father.

That social conflict and bitterness should grow, and political extremism and fragmentation flourish under such conditions, was inevitable. The Nazi Party went from strength to strength. Throughout 1931 it made further advances in a series of provincial elections. Its rough-house militia, the Sturm-Abteilungen (SA), numbered 170,000 by the end of 1931. Its members specialized in beating up Jews on their way to synagogue services, picking street fights with their Communist opposite numbers, the *Rote Frontkämpfer*, and preventing the showing of *Im Westen Nichts Neues* (*All Quiet on the Western Front*), the celebrated anti-war film.

The bolder the Nazis became, the more they were sought as allies. At an anti-Republican rally in Bad Harzburg in 1931 Hugenberg and Hitler were joined by the leaders of the Stahlhelm, the Reichslandbund (formerly the Agrarian League), the Pan-German League, numerous industrial and financial magnates, and, most significantly of all, Hjalmar Schacht, who, a year earlier, had still been President of the Reichsbank. All they had in common was hatred of the Republic and an urge to get rid of Brüning; indeed, it was significant that so many 'Establishment' figures who might have sympathized with Brüning's style of government now regarded him as the source of current disasters.

But the Harzburg Front was an unequal alliance, growing more unequal every day. The Conservatives knew they could get nowhere without Hitler, though they deluded themselves that they could dispose of him once his usefulness was over. Hitler, now committed to gaining power legally, needed them only as long as he felt he was short of a majority himself. In their vilification of the Republic, in their demands for a total repudiation of Versailles, in their demagogy, frequently in their anti-Semitism, the older groups in no way lagged behind the Nazis. But however much they might always have hated the Republic, they had co-operated with it when times were good. Too many of them were associated with monarchy and its taint of failure. Their public image was that of has-beens. The Nazis, on the other hand—and this they shared to some extent with the Communists—represented youth, novelty, and dynamism. Two-thirds of the revolutionary parties' Reichstag deputies were under forty. They were unsullied by the failures of this and any previous 'system'. Above all, what the Nazis could offer was what the other right-wing opponents of the Republic lacked, a mass following. Hitler lost no opportunity of ingratiating himself with those who controlled influence or funds, culminating in his crucial address to the exclusive Industrie-Klub of Düsseldorf in January 1932, in which he pledged respect for private property. Equally the Nazis needed to maintain the radicalism of their mass constituency at full pitch, to the extent even of supporting strikes in places where the Communists were the chief rival, and of blackmailing their Junker patrons over the *Osthilfe* scandals.

The fragility of the Harzburg alliance was shown by the Presidential election of April 1932. Hindenburg had been elected in 1925 as the trump card of the Right. So far had fortunes changed that he was now, though semi-senile, the moderates' last hope against subversion. The 'Weimar' parties nominated him as their joint candidate. Against him the Stahlhelm put up one of their officials to represent the self-styled 'national opposition', only to find themselves outflanked by Hitler's own intervention. Hindenburg was re-elected only in the second round, having failed to gain an absolute majority. He finally got 53 per cent of the vote, Hitler 37 per cent, the Communist Thälmann 10 per cent. Later the same month the Nazis plus Communists gained an absolute majority in Prussia, the last Republican stronghold, though since the new Landtag was incapable of agreeing on a new government, the Social Democrat Otto Braun remained Prime Minister.

But the full extent of the old Right's disappearance as an electoral force was demonstrated in the Reichstag election of July, when the Nazis repeated their triumph of April and became the largest party. As in 1930 they made no headway against the Catholic parties, who indeed also increased their poll, and little against the Left, though further Communist advances reflected the alarming polarization of opinion. The forces which all but disappeared from public life were those of middle-class Liberalism and moderate Conservatism, of regional and occupational particularism. The Nazis had become their spokesmen, as well as of many former non-voters now mobilized by the hysteria of crisis and extremism. For all their talk of change the Nazis were the articulators of fear, not hope. The areas in which they did best were almost exclusively those with an archaic social structure—Schleswig-Holstein, East Prussia, Pomerania, and Lower Silesia. With few exceptions they did badly in the big cities, in areas of heavy industry, or in the Catholic South and West.

By this time Brüning was no longer Chancellor. Though Hindenburg owed his re-election to him more than anyone else, he dismissed him a month later, mainly at the instance of the agrarian caucus round his son, who feared that Brüning would insist on land reform in return for continued *Osthilfe*. Yet if Brüning's power base was narrow, that of his successors, Franz von Papen and General Kurt von Schleicher, was narrower still. One of Brüning's last acts, taken in concert with his Defence Minister, General Groener, was to put a ban on the SA: it was this unwillingness on his part to come to terms with Nazism as an ally, however temporary, against the Republic and the rise of Communism that exasperated men like Papen and Schleicher.

By bringing Hitler's followers into a broad alliance of patriots and loyalists they hoped to cure them of their excesses and use them to undo the shame, domestic and foreign, of 1918. For this reason Papen rescinded the SA ban and blamed the violence which inevitably ensued on the relevant police authority, in this case the Prussian Government. Their alleged incapacity to keep order was his excuse for using article 48 to topple Otto Braun's minority administration. Thus the last, and in many ways the most reliable, Republican hands were removed from the levers of power. Responsibility for law and order in Berlin now rested with an authoritarian, anti-Republican government.

Papen's coup suggested that the Republic was on its deathbed. The Social Democrats have been much criticized for not resisting it—if only symbolically, to save their honour. They were no doubt dispirited and defeatist by then, their followers demoralized by unemployment and tempted by the rival attractions of Communism. The brave days of the Kapp *putsch*, when a general strike could mobilize Republicans of all shades, were a long way behind. The balance of violence had tipped against the Republic.

If the Republic was visibly dying, it was by no means certain who would succeed. Under Papen's chancellorship the first steps were taken towards a reflation of the economy. More important in the short run, reparations, already suspended by President Hoover's moratorium, were formally terminated. But it is difficult to govern a modern state without either a mass base or an overt dictatorship and Papen seemed unable to find the first and unwilling to embark on the second. While the modest improvements in conditions led to a sizeable decline in Nazi votes in a yet further Reichstag election in November—thus demonstrating that the Nazi bandwagon was far from unstoppable—Papen himself had to give way to the one force capable of sustaining his type of authority: the army. Now began the fateful interlude of the last of the Weimar Chancellors, General Schleicher, who had himself hoisted Papen into office.

Schleicher's aim was the same as Papen's: a 'concentration of national forces', in which Hitler was to play an allotted role. It was a scheme that also had Hindenburg's sympathy. The Nazis' electoral reverses made it even more attractive: they were still needed, but their bargaining power was reduced. But while the Nazi vote went down, that of the KPD rose further. Fear of Communism now dominated the minds of the figures round Hindenburg and Papen, a fear skilfully exploited by Hitler. Moreover Schleicher was impressed with the headway Nazi ideas were making among junior army officers—more and more Nazism seemed synonymous with national regeneration. In addition, Schleicher fancied himself as a social reformer: through the army he was to reconcile both the unions and the Nazi Left round Gregor Strasser. Yet he failed to overcome the distrust of the mass organizations, while mortgaging the confidence of industrialists and landowners. He was prepared to embroil the army in politics, but not to associate it with parties or to seek the support of the Reichstag: there was no reason why he should succeed in clearing the hurdles which had tripped Papen and Brüning.

The impasse did not last long. Unable to gain the parliamentary support of any party, unable to persuade President Hindenburg to dissolve the Reichstag yet again and to rule dictatorially through article 48, he vied with Papen in intriguing for Hitler's crucial support. The army was by this time convinced that only Hitler could restore political order; Ruhr industrialists were paying off the Nazi Party's debts. The hardest bargainer was, in fact, Hitler, insisting, as he had done for months, that he would join no government of which he was not the head. On 30 January 1933 his patience was rewarded.

Hitler's was not a Nazi cabinet. Of its eleven members only the Chancellor, Hermann Goering, and Wilhelm Frick were Nazis. Five, including Hugenberg, came from the DNVP; Papen was Vice-Chancellor; General Werner von Blomberg represented the army's— and the President's—interests. Hitler's claim on Hindenburg rested on his parliamentary following, for the President was tired of minority governments. To secure his majority Hitler demanded, and obtained, yet further elections, this time with himself in command of the state machine, the means of publicity, and the forces of order.

Nothing contributed more to the atmosphere of panic that Hitler needed than the Reichstag Fire of 27 February. Its causes are obscure to this day. That it was a Communist plot, as the Nazis claimed, can be ruled out. The documents do not support it, and the four Communists arrested on charges of arson, including the later Secretary-General of the Communist International, Georgi Dimitrov, had to be acquitted in what was intended as a show trial. That it was a Nazi plot to discredit the Communists, once widely believed, is now also less likely. Marinus van der Lubbe, a Dutch labourer of anarchist leanings, whom the Nazis claimed to have apprehended in the burning building and who, alone of the accused, was found guilty and executed, was probably a loner and not, as many were tempted to believe, a Nazi stooge. More important, the fire enabled Hitler to secure from Hindenburg his signature to the most draconian of all measures yet promulgated under article 48: the *Verordnung zum Schutz von Volk und Staat* (Decree for the Protection of the People and the State), which suspended freedom of the press and of assembly; permitted search and imprisonment without warrant, and interception of mail; and instituted the death penalty for acts of sabotage.

Five days later, under conditions of the nation-wide state of emergency, Hitler secured his last and greatest electoral triumph. In a record turn-out the Nazis won 44 per cent of the votes, but even now, despite mounting intimidation, they needed their DNVP coalition partners for an absolute majority. This Reichstag had only one function to perform, to pass the *Gesetz zur Behebung der Not von Volk und Reich* (Law for the Alleviation of the People's and the *Reich's* Misery), known as the Enabling Law, giving the Government sweeping powers for four years and rendering parliament virtually superfluous. The Communist members of the Reichstag were by this time under arrest; the Zentrum leader, Monsignor Kaas, assured his party's support, partly in return for promises to respect the rights of the Church and Germany's federal structure, but also because even this once-democratic party feared Bolshevism more than Fascism, and had never been entirely free from the authoritarian patriotism that had periodically gripped the country since the beginnings of the unification movement. With only the SPD voting against, the law passed without difficulty. The Enabling Law gave Hitler no powers that he had not already gained under the Reichstag Fire decrees. Between them, these enactments formed the basis of his rule for the next twelve years. In so far as the Third Reich had a constitution, it may be deduced from these two measures. Though the powers Hitler gained were virtually unlimited, he attached great importance to the way he obtained them. Though despising parliamentary democracy, the Nazis prided themselves on their popular support; the electoral mandate of March 1933 was therefore vital to their claim to political legitimacy. Though despising the rule of law, Hitler appreciated, after the fiasco of the 1923 Munich *putsch*, that he could gain power only through, not against the existing institutions. 'Now', Goebbels triumphantly recorded in his diary, 'we are also the constitutional masters of the *Reich*'.

The Nazis were fond of referring to their seizure of power as a 'national uprising', or a 'national awakening', the culmination of an irresistible popular movement. Yet the events of 1930 to 1933 tell a different story. 1932 was a year of plebiscitary triumph, but also of political frustration; in Goebbels' words, 'an eternal stream of bad luck'. 'The past has been difficult,' he wrote at the end of 1932, 'the future dark and sombre; all hopes and prospects completely vanished.' The Nazis triumphed because many of the slogans and symbols which they exploited—those of national solidarity, resentment at defeat, a yearning for strong government, a dislike of urban, industrial civilization, anti-Semitism—were the common ground of many Germans, inculcated by the experience of the nineteenth and twentieth centuries, and strengthened by the educational system. They triumphed because they found in Hitler a matchless demagogue and ruthless tactician who outflanked and outmanoeuvred all those who sought to offer solutions similar to his. They triumphed because parliamentary democracy in Germany was tarred as a foreign import and the product of defeat, because the leaders of the parliamentary parties, inexperienced in exercising their responsibilities, gave Germany neither stable nor effective government. They triumphed because the Depression brought many of all classes to economic despair, and to fear of a Bolshevik take-over. They triumphed above all because, in the crucial autumn and winter of 1932–3, many who feared or despised them nevertheless perceived them as a lesser evil or as a necessary ally against the Republic that they, too, wished to kill—generals, landowners, industrialists, civil servants, academics, churchmen—men, some of whom a few years later were to join the Resistance, flee into exile, or die in concentration camps. But for the moment they ignored the warning of that previous Witches' Sabbath, described by Goethe:

FAUST. The mob streams up to Satan's throne;
I'd learn things there I've never known . . .
MEPHISTOPHELES. The whole mob streams and strives uphill:
One thinks one's pushing and one's pushed against one's will.

6 The Third Reich in Peace, 1933–1939

Had I as many souls as there be stars,
I'd give them all for Mephistophilis.
By him I'll be great emperor of the world.

(Christopher Marlowe, *The Tragical*
History of Doctor Faustus)

Once we have power, we shall never again give it up, unless we
are carried out as corpses from our offices.

(Joseph Goebbels, *Diaries*, 6 August 1932)

Consolidation

A third empire, to crown the glory of its two predecessors, the Holy
Roman and the Bismarckian, an empire to last a thousand years—that
is what Hitler promised not only to the German people but to himself.
It is known to history for its unexampled tyranny and aggressiveness,
but the apparatus for carrying out the ultimate fantasies of the Nazi
programme was built up gradually and, at times, hesitantly. What the
Nazis called their seizure of power was not a single event, but a
process. It went on in fits and starts and with occasional reverses, but
never lost sight of the ultimate objective. That there was such an
objective cannot be doubted, nor that there was a Nazi programme.
Some parts of it, like economic and social reform or the ideological
superstructure associated with the party's self-appointed philosopher,
Alfred Rosenberg, were ballast, to be taken on or jettisoned as occasion
demanded. Others were genuinely unalterable, in the words of the
party's Twenty-Five Points. The will to secure a monopoly of absolute
power, to wield this power through a racially pure élite on the leadership principle, to undo the 1919 peace settlement and replace it with a
'New Order', in which the *Herrenvolk* would lord it over Slavs and

Latins, reduced to helotry—this was the movement's *raison d'être* and its dynamic. Hitler never lost sight of these aims, first outlined in *Mein Kampf* in 1923 and repeated in all subsequent records of his opinions right down to his political testament of April 1945. In his methods and his tactics he was, however, opportunist. He could be patient and flexible as well as impulsive; he preferred, if possible, to let his antagonist make a fatal mistake.

Throughout 1933 and 1934 he had to move cautiously—with enough terror to dispose of any threat to his rule and to satisfy the bloodlust of his followers, with enough circumspection to lull those whose help he needed inside and outside Germany. The first wave of terror was designed to secure total control of the levers of political power. It came through the Nazis' control of the federal state governments, which were, under the Weimar constitution, the police authorities. Hermann Goering was appointed Prussian Minister of the Interior and set about creating the first concentration camps for the— entirely illegal—detention and ill-treatment of political opponents. He also recruited an 'auxiliary police', 50,000 strong, mainly from the two party militias, the SA and the SS, against whose assaults and robberies the regular forces of the law were powerless. Hitler used the Reichstag Fire decrees to turn out the elected governments of the states and give executive power to appointed governors, usually the *Gauleiter* (regional bosses) of the party. In Prussia that post went to Goering. The arrangement was temporary only; in 1934 the state governments were abolished altogether. For the remaining eleven years of Hitler's dictatorship Germany had the one and only truly centralized executive in its history. This initial phase of the terror reached its climax in the spring and summer of 1933. In places its character was semi-anarchical, indicating lack of control by the new regime, rather than the restoration of order that it had promised. It also reflected the nature of the Nazi movement, which had risen to power, and recruited its following, through the glorification of violence. In the first three months of 1933 there were 69 politically motivated murders. In many parts of Germany, SA gangs took revenge on their political opponents on the Left and, in some cases, among Catholics with arbitrary assaults and vandalism.

The two most spectacular acts of terror, and the ones most

noticed abroad, were the boycott of Jewish shops and businesses at the beginning of April and the public burning of 'un-German' books a month later. The first of these was enforced by the strong-arm tactics of the SA. The second, which consigned the works of Albert Einstein, Sigmund Freud, Thomas and Heinrich Mann, Hermann Hesse, and Erich Kästner to the flames, was a sop to the Nazi student organization. In Berlin this ceremony was presided over by Goebbels, in Frankfurt-on-Main by the Rector of the University, in Leipzig and Bonn by established professors.

The second wave of terror ran parallel with the first. It was designed to secure total control of society by means of *Gleichschaltung* (enforced integration). The logical conclusion of this process was the subordination of civil society to the state via the party. It consisted of the abolition of all voluntary and autonomous associations. But it also entailed the arbitrary power to exclude: to decide who would not be permitted to exercise a particular profession or trade. The Law for the Restoration of the Professional Public Service of 4 April provided for the dismissal of any civil servant who was 'of non-Aryan descent' or who could not guarantee unconditional support for the National Socialist state. Discrimination was not restricted to the state service. Jewish and Communist lawyers were debarred from practising and the health insurance bodies were obliged to dismiss Jewish doctors. The first to suffer from *Gleichschaltung* were the trade unions, whose buildings were seized, leaders arrested, and members compulsorily recruited into the German Labour Front (Deutsche Arbeitsfront: DAF) under Robert Ley. Next to follow was the SPD, first persecuted and then banned, much as the Communists had been after the Reichstag Fire. The remaining political parties took the hint, and dissolved themselves, though not before Hitler's coalition partners, the DNVP, had suffered the indignity of occupation by storm troopers. By the middle of July the Nazi Party was the only political party in the country. The Law for Ensuring the Unity of Party and State of 1 December named the NSDAP 'the bearer of the German concept of the state' and 'indissolubly linked' with it.

Hand in hand with terror and *Gleichschaltung* went conciliation, especially of the more conservative forces. By the beginning of August the 'auxiliary police' forces had been disbanded and some of the concentration camp detainees released. The first wave of civil service purges was completed. Acts of arbitrary injustice, excusable in the heat of the revolution, would arouse the suspicions of Hitler's allies if indefinitely escalated. The autonomy of industrial, commercial, and agricultural interest groups was, like that of the trade unions, abolished, but the economic claims of these interests were not seriously damaged. Though the radicals in the Nazi Party, representing small tradesmen and subsistence farmers, might rail against big business, landowners, and chain stores, and demand reduced mortgage rates, nothing was done to satisfy them beyond a temporary campaign to boycott department stores. Hjalmar Schacht was back as President of the Reichsbank, firmly opposed to any sentimentality towards the inefficient. Moreover, Hitler was disinclined to antagonize industry and finance, whose expertise and goodwill he needed for his programme of rearmament and economic revival. The new head of the National Federation of German Industry (*Reichsverband der deutschen Industrie*) was no less a representative of the old order than Gustav Krupp von Bohlen and Halbach.

Similarly Hitler had some success in mollifying the Churches. The pagan, racial creed of Nazism, demanding total subordination to the wishes of the dictator, was in the last resort incompatible with Christianity and in private Hitler did not disguise his contempt for the Churches. Yet he bore in mind the fatal effect on German national unity of Bismarck's attempts to force the Catholic Church into submission, and was encouraged by the Italian precedent of the Lateran Pacts of 1929, through which Mussolini had made his peace with the Vatican. German Catholic leaders had already shown, by their suppport for the Enabling Bill, that they were willing to meet the new regime halfway. In July 1933, shortly after the Zentrum's disbandment, the Vatican signed a Concordat with Hitler's Government. In return for abstaining from politics, the Catholic Church gained generous guarantees for parochial and educational independence.

The Protestant Churches were, on the face of it, even easier to deal with. Unlike the Catholics, they had never reconciled themselves with the Republic; unlike the Catholics they were quite heavily infiltrated with Nazi sympathizers. In particular, a sect known as the Deutsche Christen showed a strong *völkisch* ideology, including a dislike of the traditional Lutheran emphasis on the 'Jewish' Old Testament. Helped by heavy Nazi pressure, the Deutsche Christen got one of their leaders, the army chaplain Ludwig Müller, elected to the newly created post of *Reichsbischof* by a special synod.

Nazi domination of the Churches was never complete, however. The Concordat notwithstanding, many party organs continued to harass Catholic organizations and individuals, particularly youth leaders, and party members were encouraged to leave the Church. By the end of the year Cardinal Faulhaber of Munich was preaching his famous Advent sermons against Nazi racialist doctrine. Among Protestants those who disapproved not only of the way Müller had been appointed but of other Government acts, such as the application of 'racial' tests to the clergy, grouped themselves round the former submarine hero, Pastor Martin Niemoeller, eventually to form the Bekennende Kirche, the Confessing Church. Though Hitler was forced to drop Müller after a time, the Confessing Church itself remained a small minority. The majority of churchmen were also German patriots, dazzled by Hitler's promise of national regeneration. The emphasis that he put on a crusade against Bolshevism held many back from expressing their discontent too firmly.

The most important of the groups Hitler had to appease was the army. He did so early and spectacularly, two days before the passage of the Enabling Bill when, in the Memorial Church at Potsdam, in the presence of President Hindenburg, the Crown Prince, and a full complement of field marshals he apostrophized 'the marriage between the symbols of ancient greatness and youthful strength'. But Hindenburg's crucial influence, and General Blomberg's presence in the cabinet, were a constant reminder of how vulnerable he was to the army's displeasure. Moreover, he needed the generals as much as he needed the industrialists if his ambitions for Germany were not to remain dreams. The army, in turn, demanded a showdown with the radical wing of the Nazi Party, which Hitler could not in the long run evade: a showdown not so much with the economic cranks as with the SA.

The SA, now numbering over half a million, represented the

rowdy, semi-criminal element of the Nazi movement. Borne along by envy and social resentment, they talked increasingly of a 'second revolution'. By this they meant the overthrow of the existing social dominance by the wealthy, the educated, and the respectable and, more specifically, their ambition to replace the old, 'reactionary' army as the revolutionary fighting force of the *Reich*. Throughout the autumn of 1933 and the spring of 1934 relations between party leadership and the SA Chief of Staff, Ernst Röhm, steadily worsened. At the beginning of June 1934 the SA were sent on a month's compulsory leave; on the night of 29–30 June the SA leaders were surprised in their homes or holiday resorts and summarily shot. Not only Röhm and his associates were among the 96 victims of this 'night of the long knives': they included General Schleicher, Hitler's predecessor as Chancellor; the leader of the NSDAP's left wing, Gregor Strasser, who, unlike his brother Otto, had stayed inside the party; Edgar Jung, the conservative publicist and secretary of Vice-Chancellor Papen; and Gustav von Kahr, Bavarian Premier at the time of the beer-hall *putsch* of 1923.

Five weeks later President Hindenburg died and Hitler succeeded him as head of state and commander-in-chief of the armed forces. The oath that the armed forces were expected to swear, however, was not to the holder of an office, but to an individual, the *Führer* of the German *Reich* and People. The army's triumph, apparently complete on 30 June, carried within it the seeds of danger. With Hindenburg's death formal Nazi control of the Government was further strengthened. Papen ceased to be Vice-Chancellor; Hugenberg had already resigned over the treatment of the DNVP. Indeed the cabinet now ceased to play any role in the decision-making process, as the Reichstag had already done. In a plebiscite on 19 August 1934 92 per cent of the voters predictably approved Hitler's new titles and powers. The purpose of the exercise was to stress the direct authority the *Volk* gave to the *Führer*, bypassing all other institutions. The last traces of the Weimar constitution had disappeared. It was not only the democratic Republic that was thus overthrown. With it there disappeared the very concept of the rule of law that had characterized not only the Weimar Republic, but the Empire and the majority of the states even before 1871. Not only the party system and independent local government were abolished, but an independent judiciary and the citizen's equality before the law. The special 'People's Courts', established in 1934 for the trial of political offences, were political rather than judicial institutions. Only some of their members needed to be qualified judges and there was no appeal against their verdicts. With the Röhm purge behind him, Hitler declared the National Socialist revolution complete and promised that 'there would not be another German revolution in a thousand years'. Yet Germany was not yet a totalitarian state. The dominance of the party's arbitrary authority over the governmental apparatus and the everyday life of citizens was extended only gradually, more slowly and more discreetly between 1934 and 1938 than in the first eighteen months of Nazi rule. The country was still open to foreign diplomats and journalists and it was more desirable for them to see grand scenarios like that of the 1936 Berlin Olympics than street pogroms or brown-shirt hooliganism.

One of the first consequences of the purge of the SA was a rise in the status of the rival militia, the black-shirted Schutz-Staffeln (SS). They were intended to be a highly disciplined, politically reliable racial élite, the advance guard of the Nazi revolution. Their leader, Heinrich Himmler, who believed, if anything, more fanatically than even Hitler in world dictatorship by Aryan supermen, advanced rapidly. Originally the SS had been subordinate to the SA, but even before Himmler laid claim to primacy by playing a crucial role in the ousting of Röhm he had set up his own security service (Sicherheitsdienst: SD) under Reinhard Heydrich. Even before the purge, Himmler had succeeded in getting himself appointed chief of political police in one after another of the federal states, thereby gaining control of the secret state police (Geheime Staats-Polizei: Gestapo) and dovetailing his own SD into the state apparatus. By 1936 he was *Reichsführer* SS, and *Chef der deutschen Polizei* in the Ministry of the Interior. By aiming at police rather than military power he had succeeded where Röhm had predictably failed. He preferred to outflank rather than confront the army, securing the Waffen-SS as an armed unit, ultimately of major proportions, entirely independent of the regular military command.

Himmler's accumulation of powers suggests an inexorable trend towards a monolithic hierarchy of command and obedience. That would be a misleading picture of how the Third Reich was governed.

Hitler was bored with office routine, indeed with system of any kind. New organizations were created *ad hoc* to deal with new situations, or in order to bypass objections or obstructions from an entrenched part of the machine. The organs of the state were more and more subordinated to the dictates and requirements of the party, but the two were never entirely fused. Instead there arose, beside the regular, established civil service, police, and judiciary, parallel institutions with ill-defined prerogatives, their competences resting on secret but legally enforceable *Führer* decrees. The concentration camps, of which there were six by 1938, whose inmates were almost all persons who had broken no law, were under the direct control of the SS and beyond the reach of the normal state apparatus. Such arrangements led, of course, to endless demarcation disputes, but this, too, suited Hitler: it exhausted the energies of his subordinates in mutually destructive rivalries. Nor were these fragmentations of authority of any help to the ordinary citizen. Like Josef K. in *The Trial*, he knew only that there were regular and irregular forces of order; that he might have to answer to one, or the other, or both; that the boundaries between them were uncertain, constantly shifting and probably unknown even to the subordinate functionaries whom he would confront; that each had its own norms and *modus operandi* of which some might, and others might not, be discoverable in advance. For each activity, whether it was to do with his livelihood or his leisure, there was now only one, party-dominated organization of which membership tended increasingly to become compulsory; the Hitler Youth for children, the largest and possibly best known, was but one of many. In this way it was possible gradually to reduce the individual to that atomized anonymity without which the Nazi—or any similar—regime could not have achieved 'die Erfassung des ganzen Menschen' ('the getting hold of the whole man').

It was equally necessary to deprive all remaining corporate organizations of their autonomy, especially the more conservative ones that had initially got off lightly. The universities offered little resistance, after Jewish and politically 'unreliable' teachers—some 1,200 in all—had been purged. The nationalist ultra-conservatism of the student body and the educated classes generally made accommodation with the Nazis relatively easy. That this subservience would cost

Germany her world lead in many fields, from classical scholarship to nuclear physics, was more quickly appreciated outside than inside the country. The honeymoon with the Churches was, on the other hand, brief. The aggressive atheism of some of the Nazi leaders and the harassment of the Churches' social work were bound to evoke protests. In March 1937 Pope Pius XI's encyclical *Mit brennender Sorge* (*With Burning Concern*), largely drawn up by Faulhaber and listing the regime's many breaches of the Concordat, was read from Catholic pulpits. A few months later a letter from Dr Otto Dibelius, a leading Protestant dignitary, protesting against interference in Church government, was published. Thereafter a stalemate ensued. Open resistance was restricted to a few individual churchmen, who were accordingly persecuted: Niemoeller, for instance, spent from 1938 to 1945 in a concentration camp. But there were no further attempts at *Gleichschaltung*.

A relationship that could not be left ambiguous was that between the regime and the army. There were many causes of friction—social antagonism, the close links between the army and Prussian Lutheranism, the pace of rearmament, and Hitler's foreign policy gambles. But basically Hitler was waiting for an opportunity to drive home the tactical advantage he had gained in the summer of 1934. That opportunity came in January 1938, when he secured the dismissal of the War Minister, Blomberg, and the Chief of Staff, General Werner von Fritsch, on trumped-up morality charges. He followed this coup with the enforced retirement of sixteen high-ranking generals and a complete reorganization of the army command. A new High Command, the Oberkommando der Wehrmacht (OKW), was created, absorbing the old War Ministry and directly responsible to Hitler. The general staff, though not abolished, was largely superseded. Into this new post Hitler placed a political sycophant of no military distinction, Field Marshal Wilhelm Keitel. It was a blow from which the army never recovered. For almost three centuries it had been like a state within the state, enjoying social privileges and exercising political influence before which governments had to bow. Now it was reduced to being one more cog in Hitler's expansionist machine. Where the Liberals of 1862 and the Socialists of 1919 had failed, the 'Bohemian corporal'—Hindenburg's way of referring to Hitler—had succeeded.

The one section of the population which, in contrast with the Nazis' other victims, was persecuted with open and spectacular brutality was the Jews. Anti-Semitism had from the beginning been an integral part of the Nazi programme. It was one of many that they shared with the *völkisch* movement of the nineteenth century and the authoritarian anti-liberalism of the more conventional nationalists. Jews were singled out as the leaders of commercialism and materialism, of Marxism and subversion, of cosmopolitanism and avant-gardism, of urban modernity as opposed to the traditional values and society of pre-industrial provincialism. Identified in this way, Jews became especially vulnerable after 1918 and even more during the world economic crisis. Though the great majority of German Jews wanted nothing more than to be solid, patriotic citizens, they found themselves cast as scapegoats not merely for the defeat of 1918, the failures of democracy, and the degradations of capitalism, but for the German nation's failure to secure emotional solidarity. Unlike Communists, Catholics, or Jehovah's Witnesses, who were persecuted for what they did or thought, Jews were persecuted for what they were and could not help. A Jew could not be *gleichgeschaltet* (incorporated), only *ausgeschaltet* (excluded).

The exclusion of Jews from public life began soon after the Nazi seizure of power with their expulsion from all state employment and with the boycott of Jewish shops, businesses, doctors, and lawyers. This was followed in 1935 by the Nuremberg Laws, which deprived anyone with three or more Jewish grandparents of German citizenship, and the Law for the Protection of German Blood and German Honour, which prohibited marriages, and indeed any sexual relations, between Jews and non-Jews. Gradually Jews were edged out of one profession after another; schools were segregated; access to universities made more difficult. These pressures culminated in the pogrom of 9–10 November 1938, instigated in response to the murder of a German diplomat in Paris by a Jewish youth. Under direct orders from the party leadership the SA plundered Jewish shops and homes and set fire to synagogues. Ninety-six Jews were killed; about 20,000 were arbitrarily arrested and many ill-treated in concentration camps. A collective fine of 1,000 million marks was imposed on the Jewish community as 'atonement' for the murder. Following the

Reichskristallnacht—so called after the broken panes of glass—the imposition of economic and social apartheid was speeded up. Increasingly Jews sought refuge in other countries; by the outbreak of the war two-thirds of them had succeeded in emigrating.

Policy Successes and Popular Support

For all the regime's difficulties in the first few years, there is no doubt that it had a solid basis of popular support. This was due not only to the terror, though its mixture of intimidation and cajoling certainly helped, nor exclusively to the work of the Propaganda Ministry under Joseph Goebbels, though its intensity and technical skill far exceeded anything previously experienced. What mattered equally was that Hitler scored notable foreign policy and economic successes.

Hitler stood, and had always stood, for a repudiation of the Treaty of Versailles. So did many other Germans; what helped him to power was the belief that he would succeed where others had failed. The considerable concessions that Stresemann and Brüning had won did little to satisfy the widespread resentment of the treaty and Germany's status. The very first response of the other powers to Germany's new Government seemed to confirm Hitler's claims. On Mussolini's initiative a four-power pact was signed between Britain, France, Germany, and Italy in May 1935 for the purpose of maintaining peace. Its propaganda value to Hitler lay in the fact that the other powers now frankly treated Germany as an equal, without reference to the peace treaties, the League of Nations, or Locarno. Hitler exploited the new diplomatic equality by demanding military equality: already in the autumn of 1933 he had walked out of the World Disarmament Conference and left the League of Nations.

Yet he continued to speak of peace, and only of the satisfaction of Germany's just demands. As long as the victor powers persuaded themselves that his aims were limited, that he was no more than another revisionist, they were prepared to meet him halfway. In Britain both Government and public opinion were convinced that Germany did have just grievances and that these should be satisfied peaceably. Neither Britain nor France, still less the United States, wanted a repetition of the four-year slaughter of 1914–18. France had in any case adopted a purely defensive strategy, embodied in the fortifications of the Maginot Line, and could act effectively only with British agreement and help. All governments shared the hope that what Hitler had ranted while in opposition would be modified by the realities of political power.

That was their biggest miscalculation. Hitler's aims were not limited and he was not just another revisionist. He despised the *Grenzpolitik* (border politics) of the bourgeois nationalists: his was *Raumpolitik* (the politics of space), the reshaping of continents, not the shifting of frontier posts. He was not interested in restoring the frontiers of 1914. As far as he was concerned Bismarck had not unified the German nation: by excluding the ten million Germans of the Habsburg Monarchy, now living in Austria and Czechoslovakia, he had driven a wedge into it. Hitler came from the pan-German lower middle class of provincial Austria: he wanted the Germany of 1848, not of 1871. No wonder the writer Ernst Niekisch dubbed him 're-venge for Königgrätz'. Hitler also disavowed the cardinal item in the conventional revisionist policy, alliance with Soviet Russia. The Bolsheviks he regarded as part of the world Jewish conspiracy, Russians as subhumans. Instead he sought allies with whom he could share a cause. Fascist Italy was the obvious candidate, and for the benefit of this alliance the 300,000 oppressed ethnic Germans of the South Tyrol were exempted from his crusade of liberation.

Though Hitler's aims were unchanged, his timetable was flexible. He compensated for his breach with Russia with a non-aggression pact with Poland in 1934, though Poland, too, was an intended victim. But by drawing a former ally of France, and an important link in France's Eastern European security belt, into his orbit, he struck a further blow at the Versailles system.

Hitler's first major success in 'liberating' Germans was the cheapest. The population of the Saar territory was, according to the Versailles Treaty, due to vote on its future in 1935, after fifteen years of League administration and French economic dominance. That such a vote would favour reunion with Germany seemed highly probable;

but the Nazis turned the plebiscite into a major propaganda feat, and the 90 per cent vote in favour of reunion, despite the strength of Catholicism and trade unionism, was undoubtedly a triumph.

By 1935 Hitler also felt ready to repudiate the military clauses of the Versailles Treaty and to announce conscription and full rearmament. The effect of these developments was to force Soviet Russia into seeking Western allies. Russia joined the League of Nations, an act symbolizing a new commitment to collective security against revisionist aggressors, and signed pacts with France and Czechoslovakia, the most reliable of France's remaining Eastern European outposts. As a counter-blow Hitler decided in March 1936 on a military reoccupation of the Rhineland, which Allied troops had vacated in 1930 but which was to remain, under the treaty, demilitarized. The operation was his boldest bluff yet. He had, as we now know, given orders for immediate withdrawal in the event of any French counter-move. But France was without a government and unwilling to act without British support, and the British Government saw no reason to intervene as long as no international frontiers were violated. Indeed, Britain had already responded to Hitler's rearmament policy by signing a naval agreement which allowed for a greatly expanded German fleet, though maintaining British numerical superiority.

Hitler was also becoming more sure of Italy's support, as Mussolini's ambitions made him increasingly the natural ally of his fellow aggressor. The Italian invasion of Abyssinia in 1935, condemned by the League of Nations, and Italy's open support for the right-wing rebellion in Spain, under General Franco, against the republican Government of the Popular Front widened the gap between Italy and the Western powers, though neither Britain nor France had given up hope of using Italy to restrain, or mediate with, Germany. The only serious threat to the 'Rome-Berlin Axis', as it came to be known, was Hitler's intention towards Austria. The incorporation of Austria in Germany, an *Anschluß*, and the consequent pressure on the frontier with the German-speaking South Tyrol, were anathema to Mussolini, and when Austrian Nazis tried to force Hitler's hand in June 1934 by staging a coup, he was obliged to disavow them. But from 1936 onwards they renewed their pressure for an *Anschluß*, abetted and financed from Germany, and the survival of an independent

Austrian state became even more questionable. By the spring of 1938 the Austrian Chancellor, Kurt von Schuschnigg, felt obliged to take pro-Nazi representatives into his government, after a conference with Hitler at Berchtesgaden. Within a month they had ousted Schuschnigg and invited German military intervention. Hitler responded on 12 March; Mussolini, appreciating that Britain and France would do nothing to stop an *Anschluß*, acquiesced in return for a guarantee of Italy's frontiers. So, paradoxically, the *Anschluß* strengthened the Axis.

The ease with which the *Anschluß* had been accomplished, and its apparent popularity in Austria, hastened the crisis caused by the agitation of the German minority in Czechoslovakia. The extremist Sudetendeutsche Partei, led by a physical training instructor, Konrad Henlein, had been scoring impressive election victories: though he claimed to want only autonomy, we now know that he was working, in collusion with the German Government, for the destruction of the Czechoslovak state. Since Czechoslovakia was the ally of France and Russia and had a strong army, the risks that Germany ran if Czechoslovakia and her allies were to resist German military intervention were enormous. But Hitler relied not on his armour but on his political instinct. Neither France nor Russia, nor least of all Britain, would embark on European war for 'a far-off people of whose affairs we know little', in the words of Neville Chamberlain, the British Prime Minister. Chamberlain therefore took the initiative in offering Hitler a compromise solution, the territorial cession of German-populated areas to the German state. Since the alternative seemed to be war, Chamberlain succeeded in persuading first the French Government, and then the hitherto determined Czech President, Eduard Benes, to bow to his proposals. On 30 September the powers signed an agreement at Munich to dismember the Czechoslovak state, leaving only a defenceless and economically impoverished rump to fend for itself. Twice in one year the frontiers of the *Reich* had been extended. Within five years of taking office, Hitler had achieved what the professors of 1848 had failed to do, what Bismarck had striven to prevent, what the peacemakers of 1919 had forbidden.

Hitler's methods were simple. He acted unilaterally, always ensuring that the initiative was his. In contrast with his domestic seizure of power, he did not hide his acts of international violence behind a cover of legality. Instead, he claimed that his antagonists had broken the rules, thereby releasing Germany from the obligation to observe them. He justified the decision to rearm by France's failure to disarm; he justified the remilitarization of the Rhineland by the Franco-Russian pact, which, he claimed, contravened the principles of Locarno; he justified his claims to the Sudetenland by the Czech Government's denial of minority rights to the Sudeten Germans. By 1938 the Nazi leadership could claim with some justice to have made Germany a major power again. The means by which this was achieved caused fewer misgivings in Germany than the buildup of the dictatorship. Most Germans were convinced that their country had been unjustly treated at Versailles and were prepared to welcome a reversal of the treaty terms. It is, however, doubtful whether Hitler's foreign policy successes, however much they boosted the morale of the country's rulers, were the main reason for popular acceptance of the regime.

The Economy and Society

These foreign policy successes would not have been possible without economic recovery; moreover, the economic improvement was probably the biggest single cause of the regime's popularity. Unemployment fell from six million in the winter of 1932 to 1.7 million in the summer of 1935. By the outbreak of the war there were seven million more jobs than in 1933. Hitler was well aware that the Empire had collapsed largely as a result of working-class discontent and that the Revolution of 1918–19 had broken out through working-class militancy. He was determined that his regime should not be weakened by a repetition of these developments. Did the NSDAP not claim to be a workers' party? He proposed to tackle the problem of working-class dissidence in two ways. On the one hand, no autonomous working-class organizations were to be tolerated. Trade unions were, as we have seen, forcibly absorbed into the Labour Front. Free collective bargaining was abolished and choice of employment was increasingly restricted. On the other hand the regime offered material benefits. The achievement of virtually full employment by the summer of 1939 was the most important of these. Real wages, i.e. the purchasing power of earnings, also rose, but more slowly. Possibly the regime claimed, and got, more credit than it deserved. The gradual recovery of the world economy reopened export markets, enabling Germany to pay for increased imports of raw materials. Some at least of the increased public works expenditure was in the pipeline from earlier governments. Moreover, this type of job creation could have proceeded much faster, had not the Nazi Government, like its predecessors and successors, been obsessed with the dangers of inflation.

From 1934 onwards Schacht—not a Nazi himself—combined the Ministry of the Economy with the presidency of the Reichsbank, thereby becoming the economic architect of the Third Reich. His ingenuity was concentrated on foreign trade: exchange controls, export subsidies, and bilateral trade agreements with supplier countries, based on exchange rates tailored to each individual case. Many of these trade partners were in Eastern and South-Eastern Europe; their increasing dependence on German credit and markets gave Germany strategically vital political influence.

Until 1936 rearmament played little part in the economic upswing. In that year the second Four-Year Plan was announced: its purpose (not made public) was to equip Germany to wage war by 1940. The Plenipotentiary of the Plan was Goering; Schacht disapproved of it, because he saw it as incompatible with his own policies of stimulating production for consumption and export. He therefore resigned as Minister, though he stayed on at the Reichsbank. The famous dilemma between guns and butter was never resolved. Rearmament certainly stimulated the economy, but it also led to consumer shortages, raw materials bottle-necks, and foreign exchange problems. Thus the Plan fell short of its targets and Germany was, at the outbreak of the war, a long way from self-sufficiency in strategic materials. Ironically, the search for autarky, designed for a war economy, made aggression more desirable and more likely.

Schacht's chief contribution was in the shape he gave to economic activity. The need to increase production and keep down prices led, necessarily, to policies that favoured large rather than small enterprises. The only legislative sop to the Nazi mystique of blood and soil was the Farm Inheritance Law, which prohibited the subdivision and, under certain circumstances, the sale of viable farmsteads under 300 acres (about a third of all agricultural holdings). In this way the Nazis hoped to build up the peasant aristocracy so dear to their hearts. In all other respects the move was away from the *völkisch* social utopia. By 1939 more Germans than ever lived in big cities and worked in large-scale industry. More women than ever were in employment instead of minding *Kinder, Kirche und Küche* (children, church, and kitchen). The class struggles and interest group conflicts which characterize a pluralistic, liberal society and which the Nazis hoped to abolish were merely bureaucratized. The new, party-dominated economic organizations fought out their rivalries through the combativeness and mutual distrust of the various sections of the party leadership. Neither the economy nor society was thoroughly transformed. In so far as changes did take place, they were in the direction of modernization and occupational mobility: an acceleration of the trends under the Empire and the Weimar Republic, an assimilation with the advanced industrial societies of the West. The propaganda of *Volksgemeinschaft* (national community), *schaffende Stände* (creative classes), *Kraft durch Freude* (Strength through Joy) might disguise this fact, but could not alter it.

The conciliation of the working class was never total. Opposition and clandestine propaganda were never entirely eliminated. On the one occasion on which the regime risked works council elections, the single Nazi list elicited a turn-out of only 50 per cent. But just as enthusiasm for the regime was limited, so was overt discontent. The regime offered some benefits in kind, such as child care, leisure activities, and holidays, provided by the Strength through Joy organization. These and the economic recovery lent the propaganda of 'national community' some credibility, while the regime's promotion of individual achievement led to a desolidarization of the work-force. The exiled SPD, which maintained an effective underground intelligence network, noted with dismay in 1937 that 'petty bourgeois tendencies among a part of the workers were greater than we had previously been inclined to recognize.'

7 The Third Reich at War, 1939–1945

These men who in their relations with each other find so many new ways of manifesting consideration, self-control, delicacy, loyalty, pride, and friendship, these men are in reference to what is outside their circle . . . not much better than beasts of prey, which have been let loose. There they enjoy freedom from all social control, they feel that in the wilderness they can give vent with impunity to that tension which is produced by enclosure and imprisonment in the peace of society, they *revert* to the innocence of the beast-of-prey conscience, like jubilant monsters, who perhaps come from a ghostly bout of murder, arson, rape, and torture, with bravado and a moral equanimity, as though merely some wild student's prank had been played, perfectly convinced that the poets now have an ample theme to sing and celebrate. It is impossible not to recognize at the core of all these aristocratic races the beast of prey; the magnificent *blonde brute*, avidly rampant for spoil and victory.

(Friedrich Nietzsche, *The Genealogy of Morals*, 1887)

death is a master from Germany his eyes are blue
he strikes you with leaden bullets his aim is true

(Paul Celan, *Death Fugue*, 1952)

It was with the outbreak of war on 1 September 1939 that the Third Reich came truly into its own. Up to that day Nazi policy had proceeded by fits and starts. In foreign policy dawn raids were punctuated by long intervals of apparent reasonableness. At home, while the screw of repression tightened in the long term, it was on occasion relaxed, especially when the need to appease foreign opinion or respond to economic pressures made this advisable. From 1938 onwards, as war became more likely, the rate of aggressive expansion abroad and repression at home escalated. Once Europe was enveloped in war, the last inhibitions were dropped and all limits to terror disappeared.

Military Expansion

The Munich Agreement of September 1938 had marked the climax of the Western powers' policy of appeasing Hitler. Each side publicly claimed that Munich would form the base of peace in Europe; each side took out insurance policies against the opposite happening. Both sides stepped up their rearmament programme, though the gap between them was not reduced. Up to and including Munich, appeasement seemed justified by the character of Germany's demands. The Rhineland, equal armaments, Austria, the Sudeten lands—each could be defended as a move to rectify a genuine injustice, to restore a balance that had been upset at Versailles. It Hitler meant what he said at Munich, that he had no further territorial demands, appeasement would remain justified; the permanent discredit of appeasement began in March 1939, when Hitler took advantage of growing internal difficulties in Czechoslovakia and sent his troops into Prague. What had remained of Bohemia and Moravia became a '*Reich* protectorate'; Slovakia, to the east, became a puppet republic, nominally independent.

If Hitler did indeed have territorial demands beyond these, they would most probably be at the expense of Poland: perhaps merely to recover the port of Danzig, to seize back the industries of Upper Silesia, to abolish the 'corridor' to the sea that divided East Prussia from the rest of the *Reich*; perhaps, on the other hand, to turn Poland into another '*Reich* protectorate'. The British Government responded to the occupation of Prague by offering a guarantee of independence to Poland, but without very clear ideas on how to implement it. The one military and diplomatic combination certain to deter Germany was a revived Triple Entente of Britain, France, and Russia; yet the British Government was reluctant to involve itself in a close alliance with the Soviet Union, while Poland and Romania, the states most threatened by German expansion, refused to let Russian armies on to their territories, even in the event of war. Stalin thus became increasingly impatient with Western hesitations; suspecting the West of wishing to deflect Hitler's aggressiveness to the East, he moved first, hoping to deflect it in the opposite direction. Stalin's conclusions were welcome to Hitler, who had in no way changed his views on Communism or the racial inferiority of the Slavs, but who saw that with Russia neutralized a Western guarantee to Poland was worthless. On 23 August a Nazi-Soviet non-aggression pact was signed, with a secret clause recognizing Soviet rights in the Baltic states and the eastern half of a partitioned Poland.

The newly gained Soviet complaisance enabled Hitler to step up the pressure on Poland for the return of Danzig; the Poles, having concluded from Czech experience that concessions to Hitler were useless, refused to budge. So Danzig became the occasion for the outbreak of the Second World War. German troops crossed the frontier on 1 September; a British ultimatum, demanding a withdrawal, expired unanswered on 3 September. France, restrained by the British for twenty years from acting against Germany, was now propelled by Chamberlain's initiative. The Western powers' declarations of war did not save Poland, but they showed that there was a limit to appeasement.

Hitler rightly calculated that Anglo-French entry into the war would make little difference to his short-term plans. Neither militarily nor economically nor politically was Germany ready for total war in 1939. Not only was the Four-Year Plan behind schedule, but all Germany's preparations were dominated by the need to avoid the type of conflict which had worn her down in 1914–18. This time Germany was to succeed in dealing the initial, shattering blow that had eluded her in August 1914, and her equipment—armour, motorized infantry, dive-bombers—was designed for the conduct of a lightning war, a *Blitzkrieg*. The defeat of Poland in just over two weeks was the first of many vindications of the new strategy.

The next six months saw the 'phoney war', an interval of little fighting as the antagonists faced each other across their fortifications on the Franco–German frontier. It was rival intentions towards Scandinavia that forced the deadlock. Each side suspected the other of planning an intervention there, especially as Russia, in an attempt to secure her command of the Baltic, had been waging war against

Finland during the winter. In April 1940 Germany took the initiative by invading Denmark, which was occupied without difficulty, and Norway, the defence of which Britain had regarded as both necessary and possible, but which was also subjugated within a month. But it was on 10 May that *Blitzkrieg* came into its own, in the boldest and most devastating German offensive of the war, when her armies poured over her western frontiers. They overran Holland and Belgium in less than a week, and entered Paris scarcely a month later. The French Government, which had fled to Bordeaux, faced the increasing inevitability of an armistice and a military surrender. This was signed on 22 June in the same railway coach in the same forest clearing at Compiègne as the armistice of 1918. By it Germany reannexed Alsace and Lorraine and occupied the whole of Northern France and the Atlantic littoral. The rest of France retained nominal independence, with a government headed by Marshal Pétain, centred on the spa town of Vichy.

This transformation of the military balance left only Britain in the war against Germany. Towards Britain Hitler had no coherent policy: he did not regard the British, in contrast with the French, the Poles, and the Russians, as hereditary opponents or racially inferior. He assumed that with the defeat of her continental allies Britain would want to seek an honourable peace, in return for the safeguarding of at any rate most of the Empire. He had no plans for an immediate invasion, assuming that even if Britain did not negotiate, German air superiority would keep her militarily neutralized. In fact the German military successes had strengthened, not weakened, British commitment to continuing the war. The Norwegian fiasco had led to a change of Government: Winston Churchill, the chief opponent of appeasement in the 1930s, replaced Chamberlain as Prime Minister. Thanks to Hitler's insistence on capturing Paris at the earliest moment, most of the British army, though short of weapons, was evacuated from Dunkirk. On the other hand, Hitler's successes had gained him an ally. Three days before the fall of Paris Italy cautiously entered the war on Germany's side, and while she contributed nothing to the defeat of France she presented an immediate threat to British interests in the Mediterranean and the Suez Canal.

The British Government's decision to continue the war constituted the first major strategic frustration Hitler had suffered. Both sides were agreed that command of the air would decide whether Britain could survive as an independent power. During five weeks, from mid-August to mid-September, daily air battles raged over Southern England; by the time the Battle of Britain was over—that is, by the time the German air offensive was called off—the Germans had lost 1,733 aircraft, the Royal Air Force 915. Plans for an invasion were indefinitely called off and the prospects for an immediate confrontation in the West faded. Instead the war moved south and east, in response to Mussolini's ambitions and Hitler's suspicions of Russia.

It soon emerged that Italian interests, far from complementing those of Germany, rivalled them, and Italian incompetence in pursuing them extended Germany's commitments. An Italian offensive into Egypt, aimed at the Suez Canal, was stopped well short of its target, and a British counter-offensive during the winter drove the Italian army back several hundred miles. An Italian assault on Greece fared even worse, with the Greek army advancing north into Italian-occupied Albania. But the chief reason for Germany's renewed interest in Eastern Europe, after the stalemate on the English Channel, was rivalry with Russia for the domination of the Balkans. The right-wing governments of Russia's neighbours were prepared in varying degrees to become Germany's vassals, with Hungary, another of the victims of the 1919 peace settlement, as Germany's most eligible ally. By the spring of 1941 plans for Hitler's most ambitious undertaking, Operation Barbarossa, were well advanced. The attack on Russia was scheduled for 15 May, in time to knock Russia out before the winter. It was Yugoslavia that upset the timetable. By the beginning of April Yugoslavia was the only Balkan state not under Axis military dominance; moreover, through Yugoslavia led the road to Greece, where Hitler had decided to bail out his Italian allies. The Yugoslav Government's military agreement with Germany at the end of March was, however, repudiated by a patriotic rebellion and Germany was obliged to impose her will by armed force. Once more *Blitzkrieg* tactics paid off: in less than a month German control of both Yugoslavia and Greece was secure. But the diversion meant the postponement of Barbarossa and the invasion of Russia did not take place until 22 June—the exact anniversary of Napoleon's attack 129 years earlier.

In retrospect Hitler blamed Mussolini for upsetting his schedule, thus depriving him of victory over Russia in the summer of 1941. Yet Hitler failed for the same reason that Napoleon had failed—the vastness of the country and the fanatical patriotism of the population make it almost impossible to defeat Russia in conventional war. Although Stalin was—amazingly—taken by surprise by the German invasion, although the Soviet armies lost three million men in the first weeks of the war, although the German army had advanced up to 400 miles by the end of July, the Germans failed to reach their objective. Leningrad was besieged, but not captured. The German thrust was halted a few miles short of Moscow. When the winter set in it was the Germans who were found to be unprepared, and for the first time since 1939 German armies were on the retreat.

Two days after the Russians began their successful winter offensive Germany gained a valuable new ally. As negotiations between Japan and the USA were breaking down, Japan launched a surprise air attack on America's main Pacific base at Pearl Harbor. Japan, whose Far Eastern ambitions equalled Germany's in Europe, had been drawing closer to Germany for some years and had become the formal ally of Germany and Italy in 1940; in Russia, Britain, and ultimately the USA the two states had common enemies. Having repeated Napoleon's mistake in June, Hitler now repeated Ludendorff's and Wilhelm II's in December: he, too, declared war on the United States. It was the price he had to pay for Japan's intervention.

In the long run, this committed America to a degree of military intervention in Europe she might otherwise not have contemplated, but in the early months of 1942 Japan's spectacular victories further weakened Germany's enemies. Japanese armies swept through Hong Kong, Malaya, Singapore, the Philippines, and the Dutch East Indies (now Indonesia). They inflicted grievous losses on the British navy, and threatened Australia and India, whose armies had hitherto formed an important part of British strength in the Middle East. And with the coming of the spring the campaigning advantage in Russia passed once more to the Germans, who extended their domain still further, thrusting deep into the Caucasus and reaching the River Volga at Stalingrad. They were even able to come to the aid of the Italian armies in North Africa, and in a brilliant campaign Field Marshal Rommel advanced to within sixty miles of the Suez Canal. While Japan bestrode the Pacific and Indian Oceans, Hitler was master of all of continental Europe except Sweden, Switzerland, Spain, and Portugal, and of most of North Africa. It was the apogee of the Third Reich.

The Drive towards Total Domination

It was not only militarily that Nazism realized its potential in the years 1938–43. Politically, too, the years of caution and compromise were now over. The accelerating momentum in foreign policy after the *Anschluß* was paralleled by radicalization domestically. The annexations increased the competences of the police and the party, and the opportunities for their specialized skills. The number of concentration camp inmates, relatively stable at 10,000 until 1938, rose to 25,000 in 1939 and 100,000 in 1940. A decree at the beginning of 1938 instituted preventive detention in concentration camps for all persons with an 'anti-social' life-style. This marked the beginning of forced labour as a regular component of the Third Reich's economy and of the systematic discrimination against gypsies. The intensification of terror was accompanied by the intensification of indoctrination. The opening of the neo-classical 'House of German Art' in Munich in 1937 was the occasion for the exhibition of 'degenerate art'. Just before *Kristallnacht* Goebbels inaugurated the exhibition 'The Eternal Jew', designed to fan popular anti-Semitism, which attracted record crowds when it moved to Vienna after the *Anschluß*. The *Kristallnacht* symbolized an intensification of the regime's racialist drive, and this reversion to the aims and methods of the earlier 'period of struggle' also required an easing-out of those public servants, borrowed from the older élites, who still held positions of responsibility. Schacht finally left the Reichsbank in 1938; Konstantin von Neurath, the career diplomat, gave way at the Foreign Ministry to Joachim von Ribbentrop, the *arriviste* sycophant; the Blomberg–Fritsch purges ensured the subordination of the Prussian officer corps.

But it was the outbreak of the war that created the atmosphere in which the values of the party could flourish without hindrance. The link between war and the realization of the Nazis' most psychopathic aspirations was so close that war appears as the logical, inevitable, and inescapable climax of their seizure of power. This was so not merely because Hitler was determined to overthrow the Versailles system: he was, but better political judgement, greater courage, more skilful diplomacy by his opponents could have stopped him in his path. Nor was it because under Nazism the pre-1914 pan-German dream of European hegemony was revived, with its promise of plunder and slave labour for industrialists and landowners: this explains the popularity of Hitler's course of action, not why he embarked on it in the first place. War was the apotheosis of the Nazis' pseudo-Darwinian belief that life was a struggle for the survival of the fittest, of their dedication to the 'leadership principle' at all levels, of their insistence on the total mobilization, the total politicization, the total integration into their movement of every aspect of social, economic, intellectual, and private life. The growth of internal tyranny after the outbreak of war is therefore not to be explained merely by military exigencies: on the contrary, the purpose of the war was to bring about the Nazi utopia in all its plenitude.

German conquests in East and West provided the perfect cover for the private, even secret, accomplishment of some of the Nazi aims. The conquered territories did not, in the main, come under the responsibility of established *Reich* ministries; and the *Reich* Commissars appointed to rule over them had to compete for powers in the never-ending internecine struggle that characterized Nazi rule. The civil government and the regular judiciary, only too anxious 'not to know' what was happening, were early losers in these conflicts. The army, in turn, though it had plenty of civilian blood on its hands, especially in Russia and the Balkans, found it convenient to delegate the dirtiest work in the rear areas to others.

War was particularly favourable for the implementation of the Nazis' racial policies, which the regime wanted to carry out in secrecy. Thus the 'euthanasia' programme, i.e. the killing of all those suffering from mental or congenital diseases, which Hitler had decided on as early as 1935, was deliberately postponed until the outbreak of war. The conquest of Poland was almost immediately followed by a secret *Führer* decree 'for the consolidation of German national life', which charged Himmler with the task of settling Germans in the occupied territories and of deporting 'ethnically alien sectors of the population'. Above all, but for the war the regime could never have embarked on that enterprise which has given it its greatest notoriety, the 'final solution of the Jewish question'. Exactly when Hitler gave the order for the extermination of all European Jews cannot be established: the assumption must be that (significantly) the instruction was oral only. The programme began in earnest in January 1942, after Himmler's deputy, Reinhard Heydrich, had presided over a conference in the Berlin suburb of Wannsee. The 'final solution', like the programme for the extermination of other 'undesirables', such as gypsies or homosexuals, was the direct responsibility of the SS and SD. So, as time went on, was the increasingly fierce warfare against Polish and Russian partisans. Since almost any activity in the East could come under the heading of security or the consolidation of Germandom, the extension of Himmler's empire knew almost no bounds.

Indeed, by 1942–3 the grip of the totalitarian machine, not only on occupied Europe but on the German civilian population, was complete. Even before the outbreak of the war the criminal law had been amended, greatly extending the applicability of the death penalty. In the course of the Weimar Republic the death penalty, though never formally abolished, became virtually extinct. Its use revived somewhat in the atmosphere of social insecurity created by the Depression and even more so after 1933, but until 1939 the annual rate of lawful executions remained below one hundred. After the outbreak of the war the rate escalated. On the day Britain and France entered the war Heydrich circulated a secret decree to the Gestapo on 'internal security'. This ordered severe penalties, among them summary death sentences, for any acts of sabotage, including such offences as failure to observe the black-out or listening to foreign radio stations. The next few months saw the amalgamation of the criminal police, the SD, and the Gestapo into a single instrument of repression. From 1940 to 1944 15,993 civilian death sentences were carried out, quite apart from executions by court martial and the millions of murders in the occupied states and extermination camps. In the course of 1942 every major department of government was transferred into the hands of a trusted party potentate. The Ministry of Justice went to Otto Thierack, who had won his spurs in the lynch-justice of the 'People's Courts' of the

1930s; Fritz Sauckel, a *Gauleiter*, was put in charge of labour mobilization; Albert Speer, no ideological fanatic, but a close personal associate of Hitler, gained overall control of the economy; Himmler reached the summit of his power by becoming Minister of the Interior in addition to his other posts. But if the victories of 1939–42 made the building of this edifice possible the reversal of military fortunes made its maintenance even more essential. Goebbels' propaganda apparatus—in 1943 he became *Beauftragter für den totalen Kriegseinsatz* (Commissar for Total War-Effort)—Sauckel's role as national chargehand, Speer's production empire with its millions of slave labourers now came into their own. It was only with the failure of *Blitzkrieg* in Russia that total war, which Britain had been waging since 1940, became a necessity for Germany.

Twilight of the Gods

The military glory of the Third Reich was brief. As in 1941, so in 1942, the onset of winter enabled the Russian armies to go over to the offensive. Counter-attacking from Stalingrad, they surrounded and destroyed the German army besieging it. This time the thaw did not give the Germans a respite. Their retreat, once begun, continued throughout the summer. The battle of Stalingrad was the military turning-point of the war. Almost simultaneously the British defeated Rommel's army at El Alamein, while Anglo-American landings in French North Africa threatened his rear. By May 1943 North Africa was clear of Axis troops. In July the Allies landed in Sicily; in September the Fascist Grand Council deposed Mussolini and Italy signed an armistice. While Russia continued to bear the brunt of the land-fighting against Germany, Britain and America stepped up their bombing offensive and, thanks to improved radar, ended the menace of German submarines to transatlantic convoys.

By the spring of 1944 enough men, materials, and ships had been assembled for the eagerly awaited Allied assault on Western Europe, one for which Germany had prepared by building the *Westwall* along the Channel coast. On 6 June British, American, and Canadian troops landed in Normandy. Two months later a smaller army landed along the Mediterranean coast of France. Aided by the increasingly active French Resistance they liberated Paris and Marseilles on the same day, 25 August. Neither in the East nor in the West was Allied progress easy: the Germans continued to resist strongly and to pursue even more frenetically their genocidal obsessions. Indeed, nothing illustrates better the strange priorities of the Nazi regime than the way in which badly needed men and transport were commandeered to shunt more and more Jews into the gas chambers of Auschwitz and Treblinka while decisive battles were being lost at the very gateways to Central Europe.

Yet this determination could not disguise the fact that it was no longer within the power of any German government to determine the future of Germany. Meeting at Casablanca, at the height of the Battle of Stalingrad, Churchill and President Roosevelt announced their formula for ending the war: unconditional surrender by Germany. Stalin, though not present, endorsed it. Though Allied propaganda had always emphasized that Hitler and Nazism, not the German people, were the enemy, it was now obvious that the political reconstruction of Germany would have to follow the complete capitulation, not only of the German armies, but of the German state.

Initially the Allied powers were attracted by the notion of partitioning Germany into its older constituent units, particularly in order to weaken Prussia and end its grip on German policy-making. At their first meeting in Tehran, in November 1943, Churchill, Roosevelt, and Stalin agreed on this principle. For a time the Western powers toyed with the even more radical proposal, elaborated by the US Secretary of the Treasury, Henry Morgenthau, of dismantling the greater part of German industry and restricting the German economy to agriculture. As victory drew nearer, the attractions of both agrarianization and dismemberment receded. It was obvious that the end of the war would leave a political vacuum in Germany which would initially be filled by the victorious powers themselves. Whichever of the victor states could wrest the greatest influence in the post-war disposal of Germany's economic and territorial resources had great prizes to hope for; the case for preserving these resources therefore grew stronger. Accordingly at their Yalta conference in February 1945, the Big Three concentrated on more immediate problems, namely the demarcation lines between their zones of military occupation, with added provision for a fourth, French, Zone. That it was these zonal borders, and not the earlier schemes for resurrecting 'historic' units, which would determine the frontiers of the post-war German states was at that stage neither intended nor expected.

Though the Nazi Government was, outwardly at least, unaffected by the publication of these Allied plans, the prospects of ruinous defeat, and the now overwhelming evidence of the criminality of the regime, stirred the first organized attempts at resistance. Even in the days of economic recovery and of military triumph there had always been those who opposed the regime and those who had doubts about at least some aspects of its policies. From the Protestant and Catholic Churches there came public protests against breaches of undertakings, interference with internal Church affairs, and the pagan racialism of Nazi ideology. Within the public services men like Hjalmar Schacht occasionally complained of breaches of legality or the arbitrary irrationality of decision-making. Very few of these protests, however, opposed the fundamental aims and purposes of the regime in a principled way.

Similarly it is difficult to reconstruct how ordinary persons, without any access to publicity, reacted to the regime. We know—if only from the reports of the SD and the Gestapo—that there was discontent at material shortages, especially once rearmament got under way; indignation at the arrogance and corruption of party bosses; and resentment at the increasing regimentation of life, whether in industry and agriculture or in schools and universities. Germans who had Jewish acquaintances or relatives watched the humiliations that they had to suffer with concern, but possibly registered such developments on an individual plane only, without necessarily seeing them as the intentional injustices integral to a tyrannical regime. Sometimes the attempts to mobilize the population by a show of terror manifestly failed. The violence and vandalism of *Kristallnacht* found little favour with the general population. The public deportations of Jews from 1941 onwards and the ill-treatment of slave labourers also at times provoked indignant reactions. It is therefore understandable that the regime took care to keep the mass murder of Jews as secret as possible, hiding it under euphemisms such as 'special treatment' and 'final solution'. It does not follow, however, that the population remained entirely ignorant of it. Occasionally a public protest could appear effective. When Bishop Galen of Münster preached against the euthanasia programme in March 1941, basing his sermon on the commandment, 'Thou shalt not kill,' the programme was officially halted, though it continued unofficially. Other transgressions of this commandment went largely unreproved.

Despite the bombing, food shortages, and the mounting casualty toll at the front, a popular revolt was out of the question. Strikes of the kind that had broken out in 1917–18 were not to be contemplated: they would be immediately crushed. The most likely leaders of such a popular uprising, Socialists or trade unionists with roots in the pre-1933 Labour movement, had been effectively immobilized—they were either in exile, or in concentration camps, or, at best, leading withdrawn private lives under surveillance. Probably the biggest success of Nazi propaganda was to inculcate in ordinary people an overwhelming fear and horror of Russia and Communism, cancelling out any war-weariness or other dissatisfaction. The only conspiracies likely to succeed would have to come from within groups that still held power or influence—the army, industry, the Churches, perhaps even party dissidents: in other words, not from anti-Nazis of the first hour, but from men who had turned, perhaps quite late in the day, from collaboration to disgust.

This was indeed the form which the only serious plots against Hitler took. The first move of this kind came at the time of the Munich crisis, when a number of generals, led by Lieutenant-General Ludwig Beck, in conjunction with a number of politicians, among them the former Mayor of Leipzig, Carl Goerdeler, planned to remove Hitler in order to avert the threat of war. Whether the plot would have come to anything had Britain and France not acceded to Hitler's demands is difficult to say. Other attempts, both before and after the outbreak of the war, by German diplomats and industrialists to sound out Britain on her attitude to a post-Hitler Germany led nowhere. British policy-makers were doubtful whether the plotters could deliver, or whether what they promised to deliver was worth having. They were in the main drawn from Conservative and nationalist circles and they, too, wanted a militarily and economically dominant Germany in the centre of Europe. It was from this circle that the members of the most ambitious plot were drawn. They bore some of the proudest names in Prussian history—Moltke, Stauffenberg, Yorck von Wartenburg. They had links with the intelligence services and with senior generals. As their political figurehead they chose Goerdeler. Gradually—for what united them was hatred of the Third Reich's institutionalized violence—they became convinced that Hitler would have to be assassinated as a prerequisite for all other action; once he was out of the way, the rule of law could be established and the Allies approached for an armistice. But the bomb which they planted in Hitler's headquarters on 20 July 1944 failed to kill him. The conspirators were rounded up: those who did not commit suicide were subjected to tortures, to the obscene degradation of trial by the People's Courts, whose president heaped abuse on them, and finally to death by slow strangulation, suspended from meathooks, their agonies filmed for Hitler's delectation.

But if they had succeeded? That the Allies would have deviated, at that state of the war, from their declared objective of unconditional surrender seems out of the question. They desired a free hand, and were within reach of it. A repetition of 1918, with another stab-in-the-back legend, was not inviting. To many on the Allied side the plotters appeared as nationalists and militarists who opposed Hitler only because he was losing the war. Their naïve proposals for Germany's post-war frontiers—those of 1914, plus Austria, the Sudetenland, and South Tyrol—confirmed these suspicions.

The war lasted nine months longer. On the home front the sacrifices increased daily, though still mild in comparison with the sufferings of the occupied populations. When Goebbels threw out the challenge, in a speech in the Berlin Sportpalast in February 1943, 'Do you want total war?', the captive audience roared back, 'Yes!' We may be certain that by that time the bulk of the German people wanted nothing less, but they were stuck in it with no visible escape. As part of the total war effort women, who up to then had been relegated to domestic duties and childbearing, were called up for war work. Fifteen-year-olds were mobilized for anti-aircraft duties. Paid holidays were abolished and the working week raised to sixty hours. All this happened under the hailstorm of Allied bombing that claimed half a million civilian lives. Yet morale did not crack. Instead there was endurance and resignation, fear of the consequences of defeat rather than hope for some last-minute miracle. Preoccupied with day-to-day survival, most Germans lost all concern for the wider picture. Denazification, which the Allies were so anxious to institute after the end of the war, was well under way in the last two years of the war. Political apathy, which the Allied occupiers so deplored, also preceded the defeat. The propaganda machine, which had so effectively appealed to the material and emotional needs of so many Germans in years of triumph, now lost its audience.

Militarily the end came swiftly. In January 1945 the Russians launched their final great offensive, crossing the River Oder; in March Americans crossed the Rhine; on 25 April the two armies met at Torgau on the Elbe. Berlin, which Hitler had intended to leave for a last stand in the mountain fastnesses of Bavaria, was cut off and within reach of Russian artillery. Hitler had no choice but to make his final dispositions as even his closest associates began to go their own way. Goering tried to take over the reins of government from Bavaria, Himmler tried frantically to negotiate peace through Swedish intermediaries. Hitler expelled both from the party and empowered Grand Admiral Doenitz to head the Government. On 30 April Hitler and his wife, Eva Braun, committed suicide in the *Führerbunker*, now a few hundred yards from the firing line. Goebbels followed his example. As military resistance wilted further, Doenitz sought a cease-fire from General Eisenhower. On 7 May 1945 the instrument of unconditional surrender, applying to all fronts, was signed at Reims, to come into force at midnight.

It was not merely the Third Reich which had ceased to exist. There was no German army any more. After the extinction of the shadowy Doenitz Government at the end of May, there was no political authority in Germany except that of the Allied military commanders. Given the destruction, the lack of even the most elementary means of subsistence, and the uncontrolled westward stream of refugees, it is arguable that even ordered society had broken down. The theatrical analogy of the *Götterdämmerung*, so dear to the imagination of the Nazi leaders, had revolutionized Germany, as the upheavals of 1918 and 1933 had not even begun to do.

As the rest of Europe celebrated its liberation and victory over the Third Reich, the German people found themselves without an answer to any of the questions that they had grappled with for the previous century and a half—their status as a nation, the form of their state or states, their place in the power structure of European states, their claim to the respect of their neighbours. It turned out to be fortunate that for the following four years they would be allowed a respite, while many of the crucial decisions would be made by others.

Conclusion

If a new, collective [state] were to be introduced into the ranks of European states . . . no-one could then prevent Germany from becoming a state intent on conquest, something that no true German could wish.

(Wilhelm von Humboldt, *The German Confederation*, 1816)

The profound, icy mistrust which the German provokes, as soon as he arrives at power—even at the present time—remains an aftermath of that inextinguishable horror with which for whole centuries Europe has regarded the wrath of the blond Teuton beast.

(Friedrich Nietzsche, *The Genealogy of Morals*, 1887)

The years between 1870 and 1945 saw three attempts at answering the various components of the German Question. Each ended in failure, the last of them in a catastrophe that engulfed the whole of Europe. Some parts of these failures can be attributed to defects in the political structures of the German states that the nation-builders of the nineteenth century inherited, others to avoidable mistakes, others still to an irrationality that is as difficult to comprehend fifty years afterwards as it was at the time.

None of the issues listed at the beginning of Chapter 1 was successfully resolved during the period covered by this book. The first issue was to determine who was a German. There were those who proposed a cultural definition, irrespective of citizenship—a German was anyone who spoke German or was descended from German-speakers, no matter where he or she lived. This definition, first offered by Johann Gottfried Herder, was initially benign and non-political, but capable of degenerating into a racialist dogma. There were those who proposed a civic-republican definition, whereby any citizen of a German state was a German, irrespective of descent. There were those who argued that the creation of a single German state would end the division of Germany by competing localisms; there were others who saw the historic loyalties of individual states and cities surviving the Imperial structure.

The Empire, the Weimar Republic, and the Third Reich were all attempts to satisfy some of these aspirations at the expense of others. The Empire of 1871 had an overwhelmingly German population, but several million Germans remained outside its borders, mainly in the Habsburg Monarchy. The question of the relationship between German nationality and German citizenship therefore remained unresolved. Non-German minorities in the Empire, e.g. Poles, and non-Christians, i.e. Jews, were citizens with equal rights, but were in many respects not regarded as true Germans or treated as such. On the other hand many Germans within the Empire continued to feel an affinity with Germans elsewhere. Ideologies intended to transcend the limitations of state frontiers, such as pan-Germanism, gained support in the course of the twentieth century and were a central component of National Socialism. As a nation-state the Empire, and even the Weimar Republic that followed it, were manifestly incomplete. The Empire was also incomplete in that, unlike France, Great Britain, or Italy after 1870, it contained divided and competing sovereignties. Twenty-two dynasties ruled inside the Empire, each supported by varying degrees of traditional loyalty and retaining at least some prerogatives. None of the old divisions within German political society was eliminated by the creation of the new state; indeed, some were exacerbated, particularly that between Catholics and Protestants and that between the growing working class and the rest of society.

The ambiguous nature of the Empire was further underlined by the incompatibilities in its institutions. On the one hand there was a Reichstag that rested on a democratic male franchise. On the other hand there were the state parliaments with their limited or plutocratic franchises, the absence of an effective Imperial administration, and the dominant presence of an army that was virtually exempt from any form of public control. The Empire failed to build a constitutional consensus, not because its constitution was a sham, but because it held out promises, whether of national unity or of political participation, that it could not fulfil.

Like the Empire, the Weimar Republic lacked a constitutional consensus, but for different reasons. Its institutions were more coherent, except for the potential conflict between the directly elected President and a Chancellor answerable to the Reichstag. The Republic was seen by many as the child of defeat and revolution, imposed on Germany in accordance with an un-German political philosophy. The indecisive election outcomes and frequent cabinet crises further undermined support for parliamentary democracy. But these were also a consequence of a culture which did not associate the public good with competitive politics and which had taught that the state stood above conflicts of interests.

It was dissatisfaction with conflict-ridden democracy, exacerbated by the Depression, as much as the positive appeals of the Nazi programme that tempted many Germans to entrust power to Adolf Hitler and tempted many others to give him the benefit of the doubt once he was in power. National Socialism offered the national and social unity of the 'folk community', and a solidarity on terms dictated from above. It laid claim to a monopoly of public thinking and to one single, undisputed definition of the public good. Great as the initial enthusiasm for such a simple solution to complex problems might have been, the Third Reich could not command a consensus either. Not only were certain sections of society automatically excluded from the national community on racial, ideological, or allegedly medical grounds, but the demands of total obedience and total subordination would sooner or later alienate rather than integrate an increasing proportion of the population. As this regime imposed greater and greater sacrifices in pursuit of a war that was leading to total defeat, disillusionment was the only possible result.

An account of German politics that ends in 1945 is bound to ask whether there is a scarlet thread leading to that catastrophe, or whether the preceding century is punctuated by a chapter of accidents, each of which was avoidable.

Modern Germany has not lacked Liberals or democrats, but they have failed to make the crucial breakthrough at the moments when it mattered. The first attempt at creating a liberal nation-state in 1848–9 took place in a relatively underdeveloped society. The German states at that time were still predominantly agrarian. The middle classes were predominantly in intellectual or administrative occupations, heavily dependent on the state. The state structures were for the most part bureaucratic and militaristic. Under these circumstances it is not surprising that this revolution failed, defeated by monarchies that could depend on their armies. The second, equally fatal, flaw of this first attempt at nation-building was disagreement on territory: should 'Germany' be 'greater' (with Austria) or 'lesser' (without Austria); and, if 'greater', what was to happen to the non-Germans inside the boundaries of this state?

Not until 1990 was it possible to construct a German state that satisfied both the principle of national self-determination and the demands of liberal democracy. Both the Empire and the Weimar Republic failed to synchronize economic modernity and liberal constitutional development. The Empire was the creation of the Prussian army, the same instrument that had crushed the Revolution in 1848–9. Under it the German nationalist movement lost much of its liberal inspiration and became more of a state-oriented than a society-oriented force. Above all, Germany failed to create those coalitions of reformist middle-class and working-class political forces that synchronized economic and political modernization in Britain, France, Scandinavia, and North America and stabilized democracy there. It is this developmental asymmetry that some historians have dubbed the German special path ('Sonderweg'). The Weimar Republic was the first attempt at a synchronized modernization. It failed, as we have seen, for reasons that were partly exogenous, above all the burden of reparations and the Depression, partly because the assumptions of the main political parties were rooted in the experience of the Empire. That meant that the Right was predominantly anti-democratic, while the Left was fatally split in its attitude to parliamentary democracy. Finally, the Third Reich saw the triumph of a nationalism whose democratic roots had withered, but which was able to exploit populistic yearnings that had been nourished by the political mass mobilizations of the two previous generations.

If we can assume that the first Chancellor of the Empire need not have been as contemptuous of political parties and parliamentary institutions as Bismarck was; that Wilhelm II need not have been as devoted as he was to military bombast and as deaf to reasonable advice as he turned out to be; that more skilful diplomacy might have prevented the outbreak of the World War in 1914 or produced a more viable peace settlement in 1919; that better statesmanship by party leaders during the Weimar Republic might have prevented the buildup of the Radical Right and the appointment of Hitler as Chancellor—if we grant one or more of these possibilities then the history of Germany in our period need not appear as a one-way street leading to Auschwitz. However avoidable it might have been the catastrophe did happen, with a cathartic effect on German political assumptions. It needed the total discrediting of National Socialism to enable Germans to accept the universalist values of the West and to develop a patriotism that is both democratic and internationalist.

Suggestions for Further Reading

General

BERGHAHN, VOLKER R., and KITCHEN, MARTIN (eds.), *Germany in the Age of Total War* (London, 1981).

BREUILLY, JOHN (ed.), *The State of Germany* (London, 1992).

CRAIG, GORDON A., *Germany 1866–1945* (Oxford, 1978).

KOCH, HANNSJOACHIM W., *A Constitutional History of Germany in the 19th and 20th Centuries* (London, 1984).

MANN, GOLO, *The History of Germany since 1789* (London, 1968).

Imperial Germany

BERGHAHN, VOLKER R., *Imperial Germany 1871–1914: Economy, Society, Culture and Politics* (Providence, RI, 1994).

GALL, LOTHAR, *Bismarck. The White Revolutionary* (London, 1986).

KENNEDY, PAUL M., *The Rise of the Anglo-German Antagonism* (London, 1980).

MOMMSEN, WOLFGANG J., *Imperial Germany 1867–1918: Politics, Culture and Society in an Authoritarian State* (London, 1995).

RETALLACK, JAMES, *Germany in the Age of Kaiser Wilhelm II* (Basingstoke, 1996).

RÖHL, JOHN C. G., *The Kaiser and his Court: Wilhelm II and the Government of Germany* (Cambridge, 1994).

STERN, FRITZ, *Gold and Iron: Bismarck, Bleichröder and the Building of the German Empire* (New York, 1977).

WEHLER, HANS-ULRICH, *The German Empire 1871–1918* (Leamington Spa, 1985).

First World War

BERGHAHN, VOLKER R., *Germany and the Approach of War in 1914*, 2nd edn. (Basingstoke, 1993).

FELDMAN, GERALD D., *Army, Industry and Labour in Germany 1914–1918* (Princeton, 1966).
FISCHER, FRITZ, *Germany's Aims in the First World War* (New York, 1967).
RYDER, A. J., *The German Revolution of 1918* (Cambridge, 1968).

Weimar Republic

BESSEL, RICHARD, *Germany After the First World War* (Oxford, 1993).
FELDMAN, GERALD D., *The Great Disorder: Politics, Economics and Society in the German Inflation, 1914–1924* (New York, 1993).
FEUCHTWANGER, EDGAR J., *From Weimar to Hitler, 1918–1933* (London, 1994).
HIDEN, JOHN, *Germany and Europe, 1919–1939*, 2nd edn. (London, 1993).
JAMES, HAROLD, *The German Slump: Politics and Economics 1924–1936* (Cambridge, 1986).
NICHOLLS, ANTHONY J., *Weimar and the Rise of Hitler*, 3rd edn. (Basingstoke, 1991).

Third Reich

BALFOUR, MICHAEL, *Withstanding Hitler* (London, 1958).
BRACHER, KARL-DIETRICH, *The German Dictatorship: The Origins, Structure and Consequence of National Socialism* (London, 1971).
BROSZAT, MARTIN, *The Hitler State: The Foundation and Structure of the Internal Development of the Third Reich* (London, 1981).
BULLOCK, ALAN, *Hitler: A Study in Tyranny*, 2nd edn. (London, 1964).
FREI, NORBERT, *National Socialist Rule in Germany: The Führer State 1933–1945* (Oxford, 1993).
HOFFMANN, PETER, *The History of the German Resistance 1933–1945*, 3rd edn. (London, 1977).
KERSHAW, IAN, *The Nazi Dictatorship: Problems and Perspectives of Interpretation*, 3rd edn. (London, 1993).
KRAUSNICK, HELMUT, *et al.*, *Anatomy of the SS State* (London, 1968).
MASON, TIMOTHY W., *Social Policy in the Third Reich: The Working Class and the 'National Community'* (Providence, RI, 1993).
SCHOENBAUM, DAVID, *Hitler's Social Revolution: Class and Status in Nazi Germany, 1933–1939* (New York, 1966).

Political Parties and Movements

EVANS, ELEANOR, *The German Center Party 1870–1933* (Carbondale, Ill., 1981).
EVANS, RICHARD J., *The Feminist Movement in Germany, 1894–1933* (London, 1976).
JONES, LARRY EUGENE, and RETALLACK, JAMES (eds.), *Elections, Mass Politics and Social Change in Modern Germany* (Cambridge, 1992).
MILLER, SUSANNE, and POTTHOFF, HEINRICH, *History of the German Social Democratic Party from 1848 to the Present Day* (Leamington Spa, 1986).
PULZER, PETER, *The Rise of Political Anti-Semitism in Germany and Austria* (London and Cambridge, Mass., 1988).

Special Topics

CRAIG, GORDON A., *The Politics of the Prussian Army 1640–1945* (Oxford, 1955).
PULZER, PETER, *Jews and the German State: The Political History of a Minority, 1848–1933* (Oxford, 1992).
RINGER, FRITZ, *The Decline of the German Mandarins, 1890–1933* (Cambridge, Mass., 1969).
STOLPER, GUSTAV, *The German Economy from 1870 to the Present Day* (London, 1967).

Historical Debates

BLACKBOURN, DAVID, and ELEY, GEOFF, *The Peculiarities of German History: Bourgeois Society and Politics in Nineteenth-Century Germany* (Oxford, 1984).
ELEY, GEOFF, *From Unification to Nazism: Reinterpreting the German Past* (London, 1986).
MAIER, CHARLES S., *The Unmasterable Past: History, Holocaust and German National Identity* (Cambridge, Mass., 1988).
MOMMSEN, HANS, *From Weimar to Auschwitz: Essays in German History* (Cambridge, 1991).
STERN, FRITZ, *Dreams and Delusions: National Socialism in the Drama of the German Past* (New York, 1987).

Documents

HAMEROW, THEODORE S. (ed.), *The Age of Bismarck: Documents and Interpretations* (New York, 1973).

KEES, ANTON, JAY, MARTIN, and DIMENDBERG, EDWARD (eds.), *The Weimar Sourcebook* (Berkeley and Los Angeles, 1995).

NOAKES, JEREMY, and PRIDHAM, GEOFFREY (eds.), *Nazism 1919–1945: A Documentary Reader* (Exeter, 1994–5).

Index

Printed in the USA/Agawam, MA
December 5, 2013